T0295756

Disruption in Financial Reporting

Since the global financial crisis of 2007–9, new laws and regulations have been introduced with the aim of improving the transparency in financial reporting. Despite the dramatically increased flow of information to shareholders and the public, this information flow has not always been meaningful or useful. Often it seems that it is not possible to see the wood for the trees. Financial scandals continue, as Wirecard, NMC Health, Patisserie Valerie, going back to Carillion (and many more) demonstrate. Financial and corporate reporting have never been so fraught with difficulties as companies fail to give guidance about the future in an increasingly uncertain world aided and abetted by the COVID-19 pandemic.

This concise book argues that the changes have simply resulted in an increase in the use of corporate PR, impression management, bullet points, glossy images, and other simulacra which allow poor performance to be masked by misleading information presented in glib boilerplate texts, images, and tables. The tone of the narrative sections in annual reports is often misleading. Drawing on extensive research and interviews with insiders and experts, this book charts what has gone wrong with financial reporting and offers a range of solutions to improve information to both investors and the public. This provides a framework for a new era of forward-looking corporate reporting and guidance based on often conflicting multiple corporate goals. The book also examines and contrasts the latest thinking by the regularity authorities.

Providing a compelling exploration of the industry's failings and present difficulties and the impact of future disruption, this timely, thought-provoking book will be of great interest to students, researchers, and professionals as well as policy makers in accounting, financial reporting, corporate reporting, financial statement analysis, and governance.

Krish Bhaskar was founding Professor of Accountancy and Finance at the University of East Anglia, UK and previously held positions at the London School of Economics and the University of Bristol. He is the author of more than 50 books and has also worked extensively in the IT, consulting, investment banking, automotive, and forecasting sectors.

John Flower, now retired, was formerly Professor of Accounting at the University of Bristol and Director of the Centre for Research in European Accounting, Brussels.

Rod Sellers, OBE, FCA, has spent almost 50 years in senior financial and corporate roles in industry.

Disruptions in Financial Reporting and Auditing
Edited by Krish Bhaskar

Following the global financial crisis and the growing number of major corporate collapses and financial scandals, confidence in the corporate sector, and more importantly, the professionals who audit them, is at an all-time low. Based on the authors' extensive experience and unique research (including interviews with hundreds of professionals, regulators, and whistleblowers) this topical series provides a uniquely accessible insight into the criticisms and challenges currently facing the financial reporting and auditing industry, and examines possible solutions.

At a time of unprecedented scrutiny and technological change, the four complementary volumes (*Disruption in the Audit Market*; *Financial Failures and Scandals*; *Disruption in Financial Reporting* and *Disruption in Auditing*) critically examine the key debates, drawing on expert opinions from top industry professionals. Together the four volumes combine into an unparalleled contemporary overview and evaluate the future challenges facing this vital part of our economy and society.

Disruption in the Audit Market
The Future of the Big Four
Krish Bhaskar and John Flower

Financial Failures and Scandals
From Enron to Carillion
Krish Bhaskar and John Flower

Disruption in Financial Reporting
A Post-pandemic View of the Future of Corporate Reporting
Krish Bhaskar and John Flower

For more information about this series, please visit: www.routledge.com/Disruptions-in-Financial-Reporting-and-Auditing/book-series/DFRA

Disruption in Financial Reporting

A Post-pandemic View of the Future of Corporate Reporting

Krish Bhaskar and John Flower
with contributions from Rod Sellers

LONDON AND NEW YORK

First published 2021
by Routledge
2 Park Square, Milton Park, Abingdon, Oxon OX14 4RN

and by Routledge
52 Vanderbilt Avenue, New York, NY 10017

Routledge is an imprint of the Taylor & Francis Group, an informa business

British Library Cataloguing-in-Publication Data
A catalogue record for this book is available from the British
Library

Library of Congress Cataloging-in-Publication Data
Names: Bhaskar, Krish N., 1945– author. | Flower, John,
    1934– author.
Title: Disruption in financial reporting : a post-pandemic view
    of the future of corporate reporting / Krish Bhaskar and John
    Flower ; with contributions from Rod Sellers.
Description: Abingdon, Oxon ; New York, NY : Routledge, 2021. |
    Series: Disruption in financial reporting & auditing | Includes
    bibliographical references.
Identifiers: LCCN 2020048039 (print) | LCCN 2020048040
    (ebook)
Subjects: LCSH: Financial statements. | Corporations—Finance. |
    Auditing.
Classification: LCC HG4028.B2 B44 2021 (print) | LCC HG4028.B2
    (ebook) | DDC 657/.3—dc23
LC record available at https://lccn.loc.gov/2020048039
LC ebook record available at https://lccn.loc.gov/2020048040

ISBN: 978-0-367-22217-8 (hbk)
ISBN: 978-0-429-27381-0 (ebk)

Typeset in Times New Roman
by Apex CoVantage, LLC

Contents

1 Financial and corporate reporting – about this book

Definitions: financial reporting versus corporate reporting

This book deals with a longer-term view of both financial and corporate reporting. We do acknowledge COVID-19, a truly black swan event, and its effect in general as well as the devastating after-effects of this coronavirus pandemic on the economy, government, and financial community. This black swan event will have a lasting impact on financial reporting in general – as all recessions and downturns in economic activity tend to change the financial and reporting rules. This pandemic will focus on going-concern, viability, material disclosures, and the future more than ever before.

From the recent past, the Enron scandal still stands out for the subsequent changes to financial regulations and reporting in the US and its knock-on effect on the Western world – the UK included. As this pandemic has had a much larger impact on the financial and economic world, so its effects will linger.

Financial reporting and corporate reporting: we believe that the two are inextricably linked. Financial reporting and annual reports (and Form 10-K in the US)[1] and bi-annual or quarterly reports, or reports dealing with certain specific events, are often combined into a single naming convention and classified as financial reporting. However, the exact definition of corporate reporting differs depending on who you speak to. The annual report now normally includes the corporate report – the so-called narrative section at the front end of the annual report is about 65% to 70% of the annual report, at least for the top 100 companies. That is not to say the financial element has become smaller; it too has increased in size, and we predict it will continue to do so.

Just as disruptive technologies have played their part in changing the world, through such sites as Amazon, Uber, and Airbnb, disruption is starting to appear in accounting, financial reporting, corporate reporting, and auditing. Disruption can develop in a number of ways. We think neither financial reporting nor the accounting profession is adequately prepared for such disruption. This is not just technology driven but also the combined effect of a number of factors. These include: changing attitudes to openness and transparency, public perceptions, continued failures or what appears to be a misstatement of financial results despite the continuing actions of regulatory authorities. In addition the auditors continue to give what is in effect a clean bill of health with a crude pass or, occasionally, fail – a black or white stamp despite many shades of grey. The focus of businesses during and after the pandemic has been on cash and liquidity with an understandable emphasis on short-term survival. This book focuses on the longer term with thoughts of improved agility, flexibility, technology and usefulness in a period where there is a focus on all stakeholders and not just the investors and shareholders.

Abbreviations

There are many abbreviations, and it is not possible to always provide their definition in each chapter. The full glossary and a shortened version are available on www.fin-rep.org.

Reality

The importance of accounting in financial reporting can be answered by one question: What would a manager or investor do in the absence of good accounting and financial information?[2] For example, how would you monitor performance? How would you make resource allocations and pricing decisions? Of course, we can argue what we mean by 'good'. 'Relevant' and 'reliable' are just words. Tying these down to numbers is a little more difficult. In our research and interviews, some analysts claim they can do this on the basis of the 'big picture', underlying operating factors, and the management team – giving a vote of confidence to Mike Ashley's Sports Direct (now Frasers Group) but not Quindell (rightly so) or AO (unclear as to whether they will generate real profitability yet as at 2020).[3]

Financial reporting is like distilling the essence of a three-dimensional image to two dimensions. In doing so, there are many differences in possible images. There is no single 'true and fair' view. There are many 'true and fair' views. Accounting rules are not an exact science. The same company with the same physical characteristics and transactions can follow different accounting policies and standards and valuation criteria and hence have entirely different profit figures, both of which meet the magic criteria of 'true and fair'.

Has financial reporting become too complex?

There is a feeling that perhaps, with all the new regulations, financial reporting and corporate reporting have become too complex, too messy, too difficult to manage or understand. The opposing view is that it is not complex enough to trigger all the possible alarms. Let's take the too-messy viewpoint epitomised by the editorial board of the Financial Times (FT); financial reporting must get back to the basics.[4] Their view is that measuring a company's performance should be relatively simple. Generally accepted accounting principles (GAAP) remain the original standard guidelines for financial accounting. The FT claims that more and more companies are resorting to non-GAAP metrics to present what can be a flattering picture of their performance.

All too often investors and analysts are forced to sort through metrics from an alternative reality, where earnings or profits are 'adjusted', 'normalised' or 'underlying'. The justification is usually that these figures give a better picture of the company's real performance than statutory results. Sceptics say they are simply massaged to show them in the best possible light. It is telling that management's remuneration is often tied to that 'adjusted' performance.

The truth in accounting is rarely black and white. Companies have the right to present their earnings in the most attractive form, and accounting standards, the rules under which the game is played, give them the freedom to do so. There is also often valuable information to be gleaned from which measures executives choose. It is time for a return to a more objective measure. In 1996, around 60 per cent of S&P 500 companies reported at least one non-GAAP earnings-per-share figure. According to Audit Analytics, a US data analyst, by 2017 more than 97 per cent of S&P 500 companies used at least one non-GAAP metric in their financial statements.

The need for greater transparency comes amid a rush by technology start-ups to tap the financial markets with a corresponding rise in more exotic metrics. The FT cites WeWork as an example: a company forced to pull its listing in September 2019, WeWork (auditor EY) introduced prospective investors to a new version of the most common metric for cash earnings, or EBITDA (earnings before interest, tax, depreciation, and amortisation). An early prospectus for a bond offered 'community-adjusted' EBITDA before taking into account 'extra' costs including marketing costs. Community teams manage the buildings, but the number of new measures introduced is amazing in the WeWork prospectus.[5]

However, it gets much worse.

1   WeWork used measures such as enterprise membership percentage, run-rate revenue, committed revenue backlog, contribution margin, and many others.
2   The contribution margin is interesting in that it does not include: other operating expenses, pre-opening location expenses, sales and

marketing expenses, growth and new development expenses, general and administrative expenses, depreciation and amortisation, and stock-based compensation expenses.

3   To get to their version of EBITDA, they add back non-cash GAAP straight-line lease costs, and then that reveals their version of EBITDA, called contribution margin excluding non-cash GAAP straight-line lease cost.

So these expenses added back to make this newly created artificial contribution margin were more than $3 billion in 2019, revealing a small positive figure of more than $0.5 billion. To a casual observer, it looks very much as if these manipulations were made just to reveal a positive figure. That said, the prospectus does attempt some detailed justification for these figures – at best, these are arbitrary arguments. One can think of a whole set of counter arguments. In retrospect, WeWork totally overplayed the underlying reality, and the management team were caught by an incredulous market.

WeWork, with its stylish workspaces, started out with an IPO valuation of more than $47 billion and ended up being nearly bankrupt before being rescued by SoftBank (the Japanese multinational conglomerate holding company) with an equity injection of $10.65 billion for a 28% stake. That investment is now causing some recriminations and regrets in SoftBank[6] – subsequently SoftBank divested itself of all shares in WeWork. The trouble is that companies such as Uber and WeWork are newer companies, all with high market valuation but which are making increasing year-on-year losses. Uber had a market capitalisation of $78 billion at peak close to its IPO (summer 2019) and had fallen to below $50 billion by November/December 2019. Uber made an operating loss of between $3 billion and $4 billion in 2018 and 2017 respectively; its loss for 2019 was $8.6 billion, and in 2020 may again be of the same order of magnitude greater. Similarly, WeWork's net loss in 2018 was close to $2 billion and was $8.5 billion loss in 2019.

As well as WeWork and Uber, Lyft, Slack (bought by Salesforce), Doordash, Snowflake and Pinterest all made losses. Also, conventional non-tech firms such as CVS, GE, and Qualcomm and older US companies valued at more than $50 billion reported losses in 2018. The *Daily Telegraph* counted 134 companies that were listed in the US in 2018:[7]

> 81pc were loss-making businesses and almost a third were tech stocks, according to the Warrington College of Business at the University of Florida.
>
> The only time the percentage of publicly-launching companies that made no profits at all was equally as high was in 2000, when 380 initial public offerings (IPOs) were recorded – the height of the dotcom bubble.

The FT editorial goes on to postulate[8] that one of the challenges has been that there is no standard definition of operating profit under GAAP or the IFRS (International Financial Reporting Standards). Often, companies report an operating profit measure, but it is up to them to decide how to define it, making comparisons tricky. The FT conducted an analysis of a hundred companies in different countries by the IASB (International Accounting Standards Board), which is the industry rule maker for much of the world outside of the US, and found that it revealed nine different variations of operating profit.

The FT reported that in the US, the SEC has escalated its scrutiny of non-GAAP measures and that the IASB is already working on this issue. The SEC (US Securities and Exchange Commission) has decided that it wants to bring more structure to a company's profit-and-loss statement and standardise operating profits through a consistent measure. This will still allow companies to make adjustments, but the end result will be greater transparency. Draft proposals may be published soon. The FT commented that this would likely mean increased costs, but these are a price worth paying.[9]

Black swan events

The 2007/2009 global financial crisis was considered to be an exogenous black swan event that created havoc in Western financial markets – some of which have not yet fully recovered. Similarly, the COVID-19 coronavirus (started in 2020) black swan event will have a profound effect on profitability, the going-concern prospects, and the medium-/long-term viability of many of the listed and non-listed/private companies. Most of the narratives sections will either only mention this in passing or will not see the event causing any viability and going-concern issues (though erroneously). This potential failure to properly identify the impact of the pandemic makes financial reporting even less fit for purpose.

The recent black swan event that has affected the whole world, more or less, is the coronavirus and in particular COVID-19 and its derivatives. No one could have predicted this, so all financial reports could not have prepared or even foreseen such an event even in the worst-case scenario for risk assessment. However, distress testing on forecasting should have shown which companies were particularly vulnerable: for example, airline companies and those airlines where overheads are high and margins slim were the worst hit (e.g. Flybe). The tourist industry and hospitality are obvious targets in terms of knock-on effects. Ex-post the virus, the financial reports should mention the impact. Our guess is that most companies will not reveal the total extent of the impact on their finances, present and future.

Low unemployment no longer causes inflation (as used to be proscribed by the Phillips Curve), monetary policy does not work, expanding the money supply (monetary easing) has failed, and interest rates are at record lows or negative. However, the UK government has relied on some fiscal expansion.

FRC and Postscript

It appears that the FRC also agree that their current approach to reporting is obsolete. Sir Jon Thompson said:

> "We are often asked how the Future of Corporate Reporting thought leadership fits with the transformation of the FRC into the Audit, Reporting and Governance Authority (ARGA) and the Brydon recommendations.[10] A system for corporate reporting underpins audit and therefore, we see this as the right time to discuss what the future of corporate reporting should look like. This paper starts the discussion: we need your input to move this conversation forward."[11]

This is a discussion paper but it shows the direction the enhanced FRC/ARGA is moving towards. Much of this book was written before a plethora of reports from the enhanced FRC/ARGA were released. However, we have managed to incorporate the various aspects of this approach to corporate reporting.

The tests

There are two major tests used to judge or qualify financial reporting as embodied by the audited annual report and accounts. For short, we will refer to this as the annual report. The tests are 'true and fair' and 'fair, balanced and understandable (FBU)'.

True and fair (as per the Companies Act 2006)

While this book is about the future of reporting and accounting, it is important to understand the quality of accounting and reporting today. Despite the plethora of legislation and accounting standards, accounting remains permeated by the application of judgement. For as long as entities are required to produce accounts for specified periods, there will be the problem of inter-period allocation of transactions and economic activity. In the UK, accounts are required to show a true and fair view. Few commentators focus on the 'a'. It is not 'the' because there is no such thing as the unique set of numbers for that period for that company. What is 'true and fair' is in the eye of the beholder.

The definitions are in theory:[12]

> The purpose of this document is to confirm that the true and fair requirement remains of fundamental importance in IFRS and UK

GAAP, whether embodied in the new standards FRS 100–103 or the standards they replace. True and fair view in auditing means that the financial statements are free from material misstatements and faithfully represent the financial performance and position of the entity.

Section 393 of the Companies Act 2006 requires that the directors of a company must not approve accounts unless they are satisfied they give a true and fair view. The true and fair requirement has been fundamental to accounting in the UK for many years. It is a requirement of both UK and EU law.

Concerns have been raised on the operation of the true and fair override in IFRS and the absence of the term 'prudence' following changes made by the IASB in 2010 during the first phase of its Conceptual Framework project. However, these changes do not affect the fundamental importance of the true and fair requirement. Whilst terminology has changed, the true and fair override requirement still exists in the same substantive form and the absence of the term 'prudence' in the 2010 Conceptual Framework does not prevent accounts prepared in accordance with IFRS from presenting a true and fair view.

In practice, management will always have an inherent ability to move profit from one period to another depending on their own view of corporate transactions. In pejorative terms, this is called income smoothing. It is all about the judgement allowed within the rules to portray in figures a complex set of transactions and events. One man's proper allocation of profit is another man's manipulation. It is a grey area, but when you step out of the grey to present the numbers as something less dimensional than reality, it is like going from 3D to 2D but an order of magnitude worse. It is about discovering that reality is no longer portrayed. There is no right line. To complicate matters further, inadvertent wrong presentation is an error; deliberate wrong presentation is fraud. Establishing the *mens rea* to distinguish the latter from the former can be very difficult.

The same physical and financial set of transactions can produced a spectrum of financial statements with very different results. Yet all can be attested to and be audited as being a true and fair view.

However, the EU's attempt to introduce a degree of flexibility for the individual enterprise through the 'true and fair override' was considered a failure by John Flower in his book *European Financial Reporting* (Palgrave Macmillan, 2004), because very few individual enterprises have made use of this opportunity. Perhaps the French idea of insisting on uniformity in the balance sheet and the profit-and-loss account, and using the notes to present the information peculiar to the individual enterprise, suggests a better way in which progress may be made. Recently, however, with the latest EU accounting directive, the situation has changed somewhat, which, along with the ability to tap into the world's financial markets, has caused a change.

There is a similar debate on the question of relevance versus reliability, and this is equally complex. John Flower discusses this in detail in his book *The Social Function of Accounts: Reforming Accountancy to Serve Mankind* (Routledge, 2017).

Fair, balanced, and understandable

The second test has now come to be extended to the narrative or qualitative part of the financial report – covering everything else apart from the financial statements. Originally, it related to just the strategic report but was then expanded to include the whole report. The FBU test is considered slightly weaker than the true and fair view, which is reserved for just the financial statements.

The then financial reporting watchdog's (FRC – Financial Reporting Council) position was:[13]

> The annual report as a whole should be fair, balanced, and understandable and should provide the information necessary for shareholders to assess the entity's position and performance, business model and strategy.

The Corporate Governance Code then stated:[14]

> The Corporate Governance Code requires Directors to explain their responsibility for preparing the Annual Report, and to state that they consider the Annual Report and Accounts, taken as a whole, to be fair, balanced, and understandable and provides the information necessary for shareholders to assess the company's position and performance, business model, and strategy.

With the advice to the auditor as:

> The auditor is required to consider whether this statement is consistent with their knowledge obtained in the audit, and if so state in the auditor's report that there is nothing to report or alternatively to make a statement that describes the uncorrected material misstatement.[15]

So as EY (one of the Big Four audit firms) puts it succinctly:

> Directors of premium listed companies which are subject to the UK Corporate Governance Code. Take note: new 'fair, balanced and

understandable' (FBU) requirements are in force. Listed company directors will have to state in their annual report and accounts (ARA) that they consider their ARA to be FBU, and that the ARA 'provides the information necessary for shareholders to assess the company's performance, business model and strategy'.[16]

Further advice can be found in the ICAEW's (Institute of Chartered Accountants in England and Wales) guide to improving annual reports.[17]
As one senior City grandee put it:

> The problem is that annual reports are not fair, certainly prejudiced, far from balanced and impossible to understand. Even those of us who are well trained in accounts find it extremely difficult to grasp what is meant by some reports apart from the directors blowing their own trumpet.

Our evidence is that for listed companies, the annual report is not fair. It is rarely balanced and frequently difficult for a layman to understand. So much for the FBU rule.
The auditors usually use some such statement as:[18]

> In connection with our audit of the financial statements, our responsibility is to read the other information and, in doing so, consider whether the other information is materially inconsistent with the financial statements or our knowledge obtained in the audit or otherwise appears to be materially misstated. If we identify such material inconsistencies or apparent material misstatements, we are required to determine whether there is a material misstatement in the financial statements or a material misstatement of the other information. If, based on the work we have performed, we conclude that there is a material misstatement of the other information, we are required to report that fact.
> We have nothing to report in this regard.

Such statements are used by all the auditors in all the annual reports of listed companies. Yet the words 'material misstatement' or 'inconsistencies' are open to interpretation and judgement. At a normal level of understanding of English, such a statement is absolutely not correct. However, when dressed up in such ambiguous words as 'material inconsistency' and so on, it is less easy to fault the auditor. In the case of Thomas Cook (which failed in September 2019), there is an investigation into Thomas Cook and its auditors by the FRC and others.
The only exception we found to the wholesale usurpation of the FBU test in practice was with some large private companies. For example, Sir Philip Green's Arcadia accounts historically gave a short but realistic appraisal of

its prospects, and we commended the preparers for that. Of course, this has changed, just as Arcadia's circumstances have changed – with the company going into administration in December 2020.

Fairly in all material respects

'True and fair' is such a well-known concept that it is unlikely to be changed much – perhaps qualified and added to in some way. The wide test of 'fair, balanced, and understandable' has been suggested to only apply to the front part of an annual report. In any case, we found very little notice is given to the 'fair, balanced, and understandable' test. Mostly, it is completely ignored by both management and the auditors (except in the case of some private companies).

The Brydon Review[19] alters the 'true and fair' test and offers a replacement. Brydon felt that the judgement of whether there is a 'true and fair' view should be modified to an equally vague term. The new term should be enshrined in law and places a requirement to assure that the accounts present a company's situation 'fairly in all material respects'. Of course, what is material is something that has caused auditors and directors many headaches over time – including the Tesco case.[20]

Capitalism: re-evaluation?

This was the title of a major push by the FT in September 2019. The FT is the publication that in our view mirrors the heart and emotion of the City of London and the markets therein contained. It is the bastion of free enterprise and capitalism. Even so, the FT recognises that it is time to reconsider"[21]:

> The liberal capitalist model has delivered peace, prosperity and technological progress for the past 50 years, dramatically reducing poverty and raising living standards throughout the world.
>
> But, in the decade since the global financial crisis, the model has come under strain, particularly the focus on maximising profits and shareholder value. These principles of good business are necessary but not sufficient.
>
> The long-term health of free enterprise capitalism will depend on delivering profit with purpose. Companies will come to understand that this combination serves their self-interest as well as their customers and employees. Without change, the prescription risks being far more painful.[22]

The notion of the stock market providing capital for industry is long gone. Unicorns come to the market to exchange the founding shares for vast sums of cash, providing billions to the original founders and entrepreneurs. Private equity capital buys listed companies, and then saddles the company with debt (often to repay the sums used to buy the company originally). Investment funds, hedge funds, vulture funds all make this a toxic mix. The stock exchange no longer fulfils many of the original roles that formed the foundation of capitalism. Something has got to give.

The FT's major theses – and these are exceptional for this newspaper – are:

> Business must act on a new corporate purpose: Companies must realign incentives and define targets beyond profits and for a wider set of stakeholders.[23]
>
> The age of wealth accumulation is over: Voters and politicians agree it is time to slice the economic pie more evenly.[24]
>
> Does capitalism need saving from itself? Why bosses are buying into the idea of a purpose beyond profit.[25]

Greater or reduced regulation?

There has been an inexorable drive towards greater regulation. This has been the trend in the US, with the exception of the Trump administration, ever since joint stock companies were invented, with their terrifying effects on those who invested when things went wrong. Not all the increased regulations have been welcomed. For example, on the secret reserves of banks, one senior person commented:

> Sometimes I wonder whether the 1948 Companies Act was correct in permitting undisclosed reserves for banks and insurers and thereby providing an exemption from the true and fair view obligation. I am not convinced that users of accounts understand today how impairments in bank loan books are audited and the inherent limitations on that process. Nor is the difference understood between provisioning for financial reporting and that for regulatory reporting for capital adequacy purposes.

However, every time there is a failure or issue, the solution always seems to be more regulation. And that may be fair enough. If the system was working, we might expect one or two outliers, but in general, issues and problems would be caught, and we would avoid surprises such as Carillion. Also, the effect of the global financial crisis (GFC) post 2007–09 is still ongoing. Cases, settlements and fines have not been fully completed. The total of fines and settlements will probably close at something nearing $200 billion or more. That is a fraction of the total estimated cost of more than $22 trillion.[26]

Another senior City grandee said:

> I sometimes wonder whether it would not be better to dismiss all the intuitive judgements and just go back to accounts based on simple bookkeeping without all the additional valuations. Just base everything on historical costs. Shareholders and their agents increasingly make their own judgements on criteria that are essentially non-financial and the possible potential of a company (as with the loss-making Uber). In my view a potential too far to be realistic, but the market disagreed in its IPO flotation.

However, there are economic consequences of business failures. In the US, sharp practices continue. For example, Wells Fargo Bank's settlement against a class-action agreed $480 million for sham accounts and other practices. We think that mistakes such as Connaught and others have largely gone unnoticed (not everyone agrees). But Tesco, HBOS (arising from the GFC), and currently Carillon, Patisserie Valerie, Thomas Cook, Wirecard, and others almost certainly mean that there will be more rather than fewer regulations. Transparency is becoming more important and privacy less so. There is a premium for openness, and the next-generation cohorts want more rather than less information.

There are several *caveats* to this, such as the impact of the non-frictionless Brexit trade deal with the EU and the impact and aftermath of the 2020 pandemic. This might imply, as the FT[27] claims that there is evidence now that the US and Europe are poised to compete to ease the financial regulatory rules – though post the Wirecard scandal we doubt that the EU will roll back any regulations.

Trump and successor committed to US deregulation?

The FT reported that:[28]

> US president Donald Trump's deregulatory drive has a new target in its sights: auditing. Tucked away on page 179 of the administration's budget last week was a proposal to fold the functions of the American auditing regulator, the Public Company Accounting Oversight Board, into the country's main financial regulator, the Securities and Exchange Commission. This is a very bad idea. The PCAOB was created by the Sarbanes-Oxley Act of 2002 in response to the Enron accounting scandal, the collapse of its auditor Arthur Andersen and a series of other financial scandals that emerged when the dotcom bubble burst. Congress forced the remaining Big Four global accounting firms – Deloitte, EY, KPMG, and PwC – to give up self-regulation and required them to start auditing not just the numbers but also the quality of internal controls at public companies.

The Biden presidency with a (possible) Republican Senate is unlikely to be able to roll back all the deregulation that has occurred. It may take one or two major failures or frauds internationally to have those financial regulations rolled back. Democrat policies may re-impose those regulations, but not immediately, as all parties will be tempted to prioritise the return of the economy to normal pre-pandemic levels. Either way, the US is likely to re-join the tougher regulatory climate by 2030/5 or so. Once that happens, Europe will follow. That said, ultimately, we can only see more and more regulations, many misplaced. In that spirit we offer our alternatives and recommendations in the forthcoming chapters. This is based on our combined knowledge and the evidence provided to us plus our own original research and analysis, including what we have found in the literature.

The Boris Johnson government is said to be aiming for a lower-regulation economy. That was before the election in December 2019. Now with a large majority this may change, and there may be a more balanced approach to tighter regulation. The impact of COVID-19 may swamp all the government's bandwidth for decision making.

Pandemic and regulation

During the pandemic, financial regulators have moved the other way and have become more forgiving, lessening regulatory controls. As *The Economist* commented:[29]

> They have eased prudential limits on banks and allowed lenders to indulge in creative accounting, turning a blind eye to souring loans. In Russia, financial institutions can value the securities they hold at prices on March 1st. India introduced a moratorium on loan payments.

Recent events

See Appendix 3.01.1 for a quick review of recent and current events. This will be updated. This is available on www.fin-rep.org.

Navigate to 'which book' and then 'Disruption in Financial Reporting' and then 'Appendices'.

The precise page URL is:

https://fin-rep.org/which-book-updates/disruption-in-financial-reporting/appendices/

This appendix discusses the Brydon, Kingman, and CMA (Competition Markets Authority)[30] and other relatively recent reports and reviews. This appendix also examines the current state of the FRC transformation to ARGA (Audit, Reporting and Governance Authority) and what reforms are and are not in vogue. It is clear that the Boris Johnson government has two diverging objectives. One is less regulation to attract overseas and, indeed, EU, companies to house themselves in London and use the UK stock exchanges. The other conflicting goal is to tighten regulations to stop accounting irregularities and financial failures.

An update on audit market regulations is provided, as well as other measures such as the banning of consultancy work for audit clients and the FRC dictating an operational split of the Big Four and others into consultancy and audit divisions (a world first). Plans were to be provided by October 2020 and the implementation of the split by 2024 at the latest. That split is now probably carved in stone.

The authors and methodology

The biographies of the authors and their respective experience and contributions have been given in the first chapter of the previous books. The methodology adopted for this volume and all volumes is also available in the first two volumes in Chapter 1[31] and repeated in Appendix 3.01.2 (available on www.fin-rep.org).

Other books and volumes in this series

The material, once gathered, collated and written amounted to several volumes of work. Routledge decided with our consent to split this work into four smaller books.

The smaller volumes are published as part of the Routledge Focus on Business and Management. The websites contain much additional material, mostly new as well as many appendices and links to many of the references.

1   *Disruption to the Audit Market*, published, Routledge April 2019
     Updates: www.fin-rep.org
2   *Recent Financial Failure*, published, Routledge April 2019
     Updates: www.fin-rep.org
3   *Disruption in Financial Reporting*, Routledge 2021
4   *Disruption in the Auditing* – being finalised
5   Website blog and further material: www.fin-rep.org and www.fin-rep.com for further thoughts, written material, blogs, and other contributions from all stakeholders and users of reports.

References to the two earlier books are made during this book for additional material throughout this volume.

Pre-requisites and knowledge assumed for this book

Please see Appendix 3.01.3 for pre-requisites and knowledge assumed for this book. See:

www.fin-rep.org/which-book/disruption-financial-reporting/

Websites and online material

There is a complementary companion set of material to this volume. Some material may be updated over time. The glossary is listed first on this site, and material is then numbered by chapter number. There is a short glossary of the most relevant terms for this book (called Glossary Short, with about 100 terms). There is the (full) Glossary, which takes longer to look through but has more than 500 terms. As there are so many abbreviations, you may find it useful to keep the glossary open whilst reading this book. For mobile devices, just enlarge the page view. This companion site can be accessed via: www.fin-rep.org.

Under 'Which Book & Updates' in the top menu, the reader can also find our comments and updates under each book, the **Appendices** for that volume, and the **Endnotes** with direct links to the references and articles being referred to – just keep your finger on 'Ctrl' on the keyboard and then click on the link.

The reader can access the two glossaries on the home page and will be provided with options as to where to go for which book. Instructions are on the sites. This site is available as a free-of-charge companion site to this book. There are details of how to obtain passwords (if implemented). Each book has its own space. Updates and new analyses may be provided. A blog may be added at a later date. Each book in this series has its own space on the site.

Most of the references are available online. So in the site www.fin-rep.org, the references are given as links to a specific URL. Press Control and left-click simultaneously on your mouse or equivalent on the link and you will be taken directly to the reference if it still exist. Note some links and URLs require fees or provide limited access (e.g. *The Times* and the FT [*Financial Times*]).

There is also an adjacent site, www.fin-rep.com, which has additional updated relevant information, updates, and new research results. Feedback from researchers, the regulators, the government, the Big Four, other audit firms, professional investors, and the preparers of reports will be posted.

Notes

1 In the US, the federal securities laws require public companies to disclose information on an ongoing basis. For example, domestic companies must submit annual reports on Form 10-K, quarterly reports on Form 10-Q, and current reports on Form 8-K for a number of specified events and must comply with a variety of other disclosure requirements.

2 These types of questions were raised in ICAEW Information for Better Markets Initiative, *Growth, Development and Accounting: Seeing the Bigger Picture*, ICAEW, 2017.

3 Interviews with leading city analysts.

4 Editorial, Financial reporting must get back to the basics, *Financial Times*, 24 November 2019, available at: www.ft.com/content/c6c258ba-0d38-11ea-bb52-34c8d9dc6d84, accessed November 2019.

5 Available at: www.sec.gov/Archives/edgar/data/1533523/000119312519220499/d781982ds1.htm, accessed November 2019.

6 S. Kolhatkar, WeWork's downfall and a reckoning for Softbank, *The New Yorker*, 14 November 2019, available at: www.newyorker.com/business/currency/weworks-downfall-and-a-reckoning-for-softbank, accessed November 2019.

7 H. Brennan, Dotcom bubble 2.0? Flotations of loss-making firms highest since 2000, *The Telegraph*, 26 June 2019, available at: www.telegraph.co.uk/investing/shares/dotcom-bubble-20-flotations-loss-making-firms-highest-since/, accessed November 2019.

8 Op. Cit., FT Note 5.

9 Ibid.

10 Brydon Review, *Assess, assure and inform: Improving audit quality and effectiveness* – final report of the independent review, December 2019, available at: https://www.gov.uk/government/publications/the-quality-and-effectiveness-of-audit-independent-review, accessed December 2019.

11 FRC, The future of corporate reporting: A matter of principle, FRC Discussion paper, *FRC News*, 8 October 2020, available at: https://www.frc.org.uk/getattachment/cf85af97-4bd2-4780-a1ec-dc03b6b91fbf/Future-of-Corporate-Reporting-FINAL.pdf, accessed October 2020.

12 FRC, True and Fair, *FRC*, June 2014, available at: www.frc.org.uk/getattachment/f08eecd2-6e3a-46d9-a3f8-73f82c09f624/True-and-fair-June-2014.pdf, accessed June 2016.

13 FRC, Guidance on the strategic report, *FRC*, July 2018, available at: www.frc.org.uk/getattachment/fb05dd7b-c76c-424e-9daf-4293c9fa2d6a/Guidance-on-the-Strategic-Report-31-7-18.pdf, accessed July 2018.

14 FRC, Other information in the annual report: The work performed by auditors to meet their reporting responsibilities in respect of the other information in the annual report, *FRC*, December 2018, available at: www.frc.org.uk/getattachment/7afae1fe-75c8-43fc-9f60-3f2a78b438a9/AQR-Thematic-Review-Other-Information-in-the-Annual-Report-Dec-2018.pdf, accessed December 2018.

15 Ibid.

16 EY, Meeting the fair, balanced and understandable challenge, *EY*, September 2013, available at: www.ey.com/Publication/vwLUAssets/Meeting-the-fair-balanced-and-understandable-challenge/$FILE/EY-CG-FBU-challenge-Sept-2013.pdf, accessed June 2016.

17 ICAEW, Improving annual reports of listed companies, ICAEW, 2016, available at: www.icaew.com/-/media/corporate/files/technical/audit-and-assurance/audit-insights/audit-insights-corporate-reporting-improving-annual-reports-of-listed-companies.ashx, accessed January 2017.

18 Thomas Cook Annual Report 2018. Auditors statement. Page 116, available at: www.thomascookgroup.com/investors/insight_external_assest/Thomas_Cook_AR_2018_web.pdf, accessed October 2019.

19 Brydon Review, Assess, assure and inform: Improving audit quality and effectiveness – final report of the independent review, December 2019, available at:

www.gov.uk/government/publications/the-quality-and-effectiveness-of-audit-independent-review, accessed December 2019.

20 See K. Bhaskar and J. Flower, *Financial Failures & Scandals: From Enron to Carillion*, Routledge, 2019, available at: www.fin-rep.org/which-book/financial-failures-scandals-from-enron-to-carillion/post-publication-discussion/, accessed February 2020.

21 L. Barber, Capitalism. Times for a resent. This is the new agenda, *Financial Times*, 19 September 2019, available at: https://aboutus.ft.com/en-gb/new-agenda/, accessed September 2019.

22 Ibid.

23 Editorial Board, Business must act on a new corporate purpose. Companies must realign incentives and define targets beyond profits, *Financial Times*, 19 September 2019, available at: www.ft.com/content/3732eb04-c28a-11e9-a8e9-296ca66511c9?segmentId=839af127-9a56-c30f-330c-43e43f9e73eb, accessed September 2019.

24 R. Foroohar, The age of wealth accumulation is over. Voters and politicians agree it is time to slice the economic pie more evenly, *Financial Times*, 4 August 2019, available at: www.ft.com/content/fd13020e-b502-11e9-bec9-fdcab53d6959?segmentId=56a414e9-1544-b801-9546-2d038c8b8694_, accessed September 2019.

25 G. Tett, Does capitalism need saving from itself? *Financial Times*, 6 September 2019, available at: www.ft.com/content/b35342fe-cda4-11e9-99a4-b5ded7a7fe3f?segmentId=9d8c66e5-f845-1254-610a-f597ecc6b8b8, accessed September 2019.

26 E. D. Melendez, Financial crisis cost tops $22 Trillion, GAO says, *HuffPost*, 14 February 2013, available at: www.huffingtonpost.co.uk/entry/financial-crisis-cost-gao_n_2687553?guccounter=1, accessed July 2018.

27 P. Jenkins, Worrying signs that a great global deregulation has begun, *Financial Times*, 9 December 2019, available at: www.ft.com/content/fc15abec-182e-11ea-8d73-6303645ac406, accessed December 2019.

28 F. McKenna, Weakening the oversight of US auditing is a very bad idea, *Financial Times*, 18 February 2020, available at: www.ft.com/content/efa3f33e-5170-11ea-a1ef-da1721a0541e, accessed December 2019.

29 A sigh of relief, a gasp of breath: In emerging markets, short-term panic gives way to long-term worry, *The Economist*, 1 August 2020, available at: www.economist.com/finance-and-economics/2020/08/01/in-emerging-markets-short-term-panic-gives-way-to-long-term-worry, accessed August 2020.

30 These refer to: Brydon Review, *Assess, assure and inform: improving audit quality and effectiveness* – final report of the independent review, December 2019, available at: https://www.gov.uk/government/publications/the-quality-and-effectiveness-of-audit-independent-review, accessed December 2019.

    The Kingman Review and associated material is available at: https://www.gov.uk/government/news/independent-review-of-the-financial-reporting-council-frc-launches-report.

    The CMA Report and its associated material is available at: https://www.gov.uk/government/news/cma-recommends-shake-up-of-uk-audit-market, accessed December 2019.

31 K. Bhaskar and J. Flower, Disruption in the Audit Market: The Future of the Big Four, Financial Failures & Scandals: From Enron to Carillion. Both volumes by Routledge, 2019.

2   Reporting theory and failures

Disruption and change

This is the third volume dealing with disruption in financial reporting and corporate reporting. The Kingman, CMA, and Brydon[1] reviews have and are still causing a major re-think of the role of reporting, and it is addressed in this book. With reporting, we have to make a number of assumptions about that direction. We liken this to choosing possible alternative rail forks.

Background scenarios

Over the period 2010 to 2020, there has been a series of rapid changes in financial reporting and auditing. Significant progress and improvement in the quality of timely, relevant and trustworthy reported information has been ushered in, primarily for several reasons:

1   The global financial crisis (GFC)[2] from 2007 to 2009 is considered by many to have been the worst financial crisis since the Great Depression of the 1930s prior to the pandemic of 2020. It developed into a full-scale global banking crisis, with many financial institutions needing to be rescued with massive bailouts (probably in excess of £1 trillion worldwide [our estimates]) and other palliative monetary and fiscal policies being employed to prevent a possible collapse of the world financial system. It affected all Western countries and banking systems. The crisis threw the Western world into a global economic downturn and depression. The UK austerity measures failed to curb the borrowing deficit. Some European countries were still suffering as late as 2020 as the pandemic hit. Unemployment, pre-pandemic, was still relatively high in Spain, Portugal, Italy, and Greece.

The still-suffering public blame the 'fat-cat' bankers[3] and the auditors who audited the financial institutions' accounts. The public believe the auditors should have had the ability to have identified and reported on the weakening of the financial institutions way before the crisis happened. Hence the desire to tighten financial reporting and auditing regulations since then. This might now have finally run out of steam despite an increasing number of financial scandals. This is discussed further shortly.

2　The GFC was then followed by at least a decade of tightening rules and regulations on corporate governance and reporting and then the ultimate check, auditing. This regime extended across the US, the UK, and Europe and even partially touched Asia-Pacific.

3　Despite this regime, financial failures and scandals continued to occur – perhaps even at an accelerating rate recently. This is a dichotomy. Increasing regulations seems to have led to more failures and issues rather than less.

4　The COVID-19 coronavirus pandemic of 2020 will also take a major toll – much worse than the GFC – and the ultimate affects will be felt for decades. But the pandemic differs from the GFC in that it was not caused by mankind and financial troubles but by a disease. The FRC has already provided new guides to going-concern.[4] An example of the type of problems experienced is illustrated by Grant Thornton's (GT) warning over the fintech company Pockit[5] (probably caused by the failure of Wirecard – discussed shortly). The knock-on effects of the pandemic induced crisis will probably be with us for some time. It has and will continue to have a profound influence on all things accounting, finance, reporting, and auditing.

A rapidly changing environment:

a　The pace of technology and the knock-on effects of disruptive industries such as Uber, Deliveroo, and Airbnb. Smartphones and cloud-based IT are just two developments that mask the tip of the iceberg. The technology revolution has led to a changing industrial and commercial landscape. Disrupters such as Uber, Amazon, Tesla, and Airbnb are just some of many examples of a changing and challenging environment. Shopping has changed forever. Paper is dying and is being replaced by digital content. TV channels are being replaced by on-demand videos and gaming on ever-more-sophisticated smartphones. The pandemic has hastened some of these trends.

b　The political climate has changed, with truth being scarcer. President Trump's (now ex) reversal of climate change policy and regulation in the US, together with the European concentration on migration and Brexit, has meant that politics throughout the world has become more extreme. (Notwithstanding President Biden's wish to reverse this course.) Vladimir Putin and Xi Jinping have become *de facto* dictators of two of the most important global economies. In terms of regulations, they may be relaxed in the short run to allow firms to survive – though that will probably be reversed in the longer run. Although the Brexit deal allows the government to introduce less regulation, the current proclamations seem to indicated tighter regulations than the EU (quite the reverse of the Brexit deal statements about the EU and UK sovereignty – for example the utterances about electric cars [petrol, diesel and hybrid cars to be banned from 2030] and other environmental concerns).

c   Finally, climate change, population growth, mass extinction of species, and many other trends are causing major changes, leading to migration, political turmoil, rebellion, wars and so on. Some postulate that we are in for a period of political uncertainly, which has led to political extremism.

Tightening regulations, a more complex commercial environment, challenging exogenous events (Brexit, climate change, internet), and the end result is an increasing number of inaccurate, false, misleading reports, in some cases leading to financial collapse. This is indeed a heady mixture. In fact, we believe that the majority of Financial Times Stock Exchange (FTSE) 350 reports are misleading to some extent. This is the current financial reporting situation inherited as of 2021.

Post-truth

The Carillion collapse brings us to a post-truth view of what is going on. Although thousands of annual reports are acceptable (but not good in our view), these have been tarnished by a few that are not. As usual in a post-truth debate, the debate is framed largely by appeals to emotions disconnected from the details of policy and by the repeated assertion of talking points to which factual rebuttals are ignored. We have to ignore emotions and examine the issue rationally.

At the same time, every company may have an underlying reality. But the truth of the matter is that for the same company, with identical underlying performance and using a current set of accounting standards, you could produce two sets of very different financial statements, both audited with a true and fair view sign-off. Actually you could produce a range of profits and each one would be a true and fair view, or even under the weaker test of fair, balanced and understandable. There is a spectrum of results that may be claimed to be true and fair, compliant with all current UK standards and UK law. The same applies to the US, the EU, and most if not all other countries. The two extremes of that spectrum would produce radically different profit numbers, especially for those firms in which profitability was marginal, intangible assets are large, and/or revenue recognition is fuzzy, among other financial conditions. This book attempts to come to some conclusions for such cases.

Corporate reporting has been viewed as a crucial form of communication between business and capital market participants, but this role is changing. Other forms of communication are important to certain classes of stakeholders. And there are new forms of reporting such as the government websites. Technology allows the possibility of much more flexibility. Non-public dark, or grey data means that the amount of data that might be reported is exploding.

The balance sheet no longer represents the investment value for shareholders or other stakeholders. Shepherd 2019[6] claims that 80% of a shareholder's investment value is no longer on the balance sheet. Often these may be of a non-financial nature. For example, companies such as Facebook, Instagram, Snap, and Twitter rely on for their share value the number of daily active users, a figure that is not found on the balance sheet.

Capital markets have lost their appeal and allure. Reporting and auditing have been and still are responding to recent scandals and the GFC of 2007/9. However, up to pre-pandemic times, the information needs of investors (shareholders and other current and potential providers of financial capital) have long been seen as the primary users of financial and corporate reports. International Integrated Reporting Council (IIRC) and IR (integrated reporting) have made valiant attempts to solve some issues but we have found that they are still wanting in too many areas.

So this chapter on reporting tries to bring all the issues together and highlights the disruptive nature of the changes. The future may be likened to a set of railway tracks with a number of points or switches ahead. The railway tracks analogy is relevant, though in this case, the forks that might develop are fairly well channelled in one of many directions – for example, integrated versus many reports. The growth of the annual report means that it is just not practical to add any more information to it without splitting it into a number of reports.

The immediate financial reporting landscape and legacy

Theory and background

A theoretical discussion of the original purpose of financial reporting is contained in Appendix 3.02.1, followed by an analysis of the theoretical nature of the present role of financial reporting, available in Appendix 3.02.2. Next, we indulged ourselves with a flight of fancy to examine what purpose financial reporting and accounts would take in a sci-fi world of post-scarcity in which everyone could have more or less of everything. The conclusion is startling. See Appendix 3.02.3.

This book assumes that there is a capitalist system modified by state controls and services. So the assumption is of the mixed private–public economy with state intervention. The paradigms of our assumptions are explored in Appendix 3.02.4. A brief review of the academic literature is provided in Appendix 3.02.5. It is primarily negative.

The FRC has conducted its own literature review in a well written and comprehensive literature review.[7]

Their literature review identified three main functions of reporting:

1   Valuation (decision usefulness criteria for capital providers).
2   Stewardship (full and transparent information allows monitoring of that capital).
3   Accountability (an account of the actions for which an organisation is held responsible in the eyes of all of its stakeholders).

Is reporting fit for purpose?

Despite more information and regulations, the 'cut to the chase' answer is no. Even the professional bodies are concerned. For example, the most influential and prestigious professional body, the ICAEW (Institute of Chartered Accountants in England and Wales), raises these issues succinctly:[8]

> Some important questions emerge from these different perspectives. Firstly, is corporate reporting fit for purpose for investment and lending decisions? And secondly, does a company really have a responsibility to provide information to stakeholder groups beyond its investors? If so, to which stakeholder groups and to what degree does this responsibility extend? Moreover, and importantly, does that mean that current reporting needs to be replaced with something radically different, perhaps by near-term regulatory intervention? Or are reports of the death of the annual report and accounts greatly exaggerated?

We are not suggesting that the annual report disappears. We think it should continue but in somewhat modified form. It is a useful document, but we feel it has rather lost its way with an ever-increasing length and content, making the report more difficult to absorb for a great variety of readers with different objectives. And this was pre-Carillion.

Elizabeth Fernando, Head of Equities at USS investment Management, made these points in an EY publication:[9]

> . . . it is the one place that management properly pulls information together to put out the whole story of the company. There will be a danger if there is no requirement to produce the ARA, investors and other stakeholders don't have a holistic source to build their understanding of

the business – and instead we start picking and choosing information, and in the process may miss some really critical information.

She goes on to say:

> . . . annual reports also go through an extremely robust diligence process – directors and auditors know the repercussions of putting out incorrect statements, and as investors, we therefore take comfort and place extra weight on the annual report as one of our core sources of information.

Our view is that this robust process is still not producing accurate enough reports. Normally, it is the responsibility of management and then verified by the auditor. Regulations have been tightened both for management and for the final seal of approval given by the auditors. Nevertheless, failures continue. Problems are missed or ignored in the annual reports. Management can create the inaccuracies, and then this is missed or not picked up by the auditors.

Elizabeth Fernando would like to see:

> I would also like more detail on the debates and challenges that have taken place in the audit committee – audited statements rely on a number of judgements and very different pictures of a company's performance and financial health can be painted by making different assumptions.

However, the issue is that two identical companies may still produce two very different financial statements and annual reports, but both may be classified as being accurate. So what tests are there?

A senior director from a leading merchant bank emailed this critique:

> As you infer in your previous email corporate reporting is a fiction in so far as the economic incentive has undermined the ability to tell the truth. Why?
>
> Directors are remunerated on the basis of either profit or asset growth
>
> Auditors and reporting accountants have severely limited the scope of their work in order to limit their liability and to achieve greater profitability from the work undertaken
>
> Boards choose auditors and reporting accountants, not shareholders and hence patronage over rides integrity
>
> In the up cycle banks compete to lend the most at the lowest margin with no reference to the previous down cycle. Credit analysis by them

is very poor and relies upon directors and auditors providing accurate information. See above.

Despite the plethora of regulation and accounting standards over many years the same problems occur time and time again i.e. misstated profits, over stated asset values and misleading statements of indebtedness. The list of culprits and the titanic failures are legion. Look at recent ones Tesco, Cattles and most of the Support Services Sector to name but three.

Shareholder activism is a myth created by the media. Rarely do they challenge boards or enforce governance because there is no economic incentive for them to do so. Indeed the opposite is the case.

Whistle-blowers are blacklisted by headhunters and the City generally, so feeding a kind of conspiracy of silence.

I could go on but that probably represents a good starter for 10. As you can tell I feel a little Victor Meldrew[10] about this subject having seen the iniquity of the system over 35 or more years.

Notes from a senior fund manager (X) at a global investment firm and analysts:

X was very much old school, preferring accounts, as they were when there were a handful of standards and pre IASB. When they were more of an art. Currently, he maintains, there seems to be an obsession in trying to measure details rather than give a correct overview. He would like to abolish quarterly report (along with the FRC). What he looks for is factors that inflate and deflate value in the accounts. Interested in the big picture. Fan of simplicity and 'No one reads the carbon footprint' currently feels it is a waste of resources to produce lengthy accounts.

FRC Future of Corporate Reporting

The FRC published their thoughts on the future of corporate reporting in October 2020[11] – fairly late for the authors in finalising this third volume in the series. Nevertheless we have included our comments on the FRC's discussion paper which we acknowledge will change over time with new comments from all involved.

The FRC obviously thinks, in their discussion paper on the future of corporate reporting, that the current system is not fit for purpose. Instead the FRC wants to recognise that the annual report is just one part of the suite (or network) of corporate reports. At the moment the FRC feels the reports that companies produce, result in fragmented and sometimes incoherent content. The premise of their discussion paper is that further tweaks are unlikely to address valid concerns. Accordingly, we (and the FRC) present a more radical overhaul for discussion.

Failure in reporting – the compelling cases leading to reform

Appendix 3.02.6 provides a commentary on failures in corporate reporting. Carillion, BHS (British Homes Stores), Patisserie Valerie, Thomas Cook, Frasers, Conviviality, Wirecard, and about 50 other recent cases are discussed.

The deficiencies of conventional financial reporting

These criticisms, following in the wake of the above financial failures, have been wide ranging and include the following points. Reporting (financial and corporate) is:

- Unable to answer basic questions of fraud and survival.
- Unable to prevent continuing failures despite the presence of three or four of the Big Four as advisers or auditors (internal and external).
- Undue emphasis on reporting to shareholders. It was felt that the underlying assumption that the firm's objective was the maximisation of profit (that is, maximising 'shareholder value') was too limited and led to the neglect of the interests of other stakeholders, such as employees, customers, the local community and so on.
- Undue emphasis on reporting the firm's actions in terms of money, which led to the neglect of matters that could not easily be expressed in monetary terms, such as pollution caused by the firm and abuses of the rights of employees, customers, and other stakeholders, so much so that gender and supplier payments are now reported through a government website.
- Neglect of information about the impact of the firm's activities on the environment. This issue assumed increasing importance as it became clear that economic activity was having a damaging impact on the environment, leading to questions as to the sustainability of the current mode of economic activity.
- Undue emphasis on the short term and neglect of the long term; there was a widespread belief that 'short termism' was damaging the British economy; this was especially a problem for companies whose shares were quoted on the stock exchange and who felt a need to satisfy shareholders, who often held their shares for relatively short periods.
- Undue emphasis on the past, with very little information about the future; most users of reports are interested more in the future than in the past;

their interest is in assessing those possible future actions of the firm that may affect them. In the words of a famous economist, 'bygones are forever bygones'; the past cannot be changed, but the future can.

- Unable to provide a short-term (up to 12 months) view of going-concern and the longer term (more than 12 months) view of viability. Recent failures have all given a clean bill of health to the short-run going concern and the longer-term viability – then they have failed. Normally the auditors – the final bastion of reasonable and checking – have just accepted the management view and forecasts. The 2019 tightening of the FRC Going Concern rule may have little difference, as it lacks teeth.
- And of course the current failure for reports to tackle black swan events, such as the pandemic, through stress testing of financial forecasts and modelling.

If there is any doubt, the Brydon Review[12] and the Kingman Review[13] certainly make it clear that financial and corporate reporting have so far failed both for a company's shareholders and for the wider stakeholders.

The FRC criticisms[14]

These were:

1   Stakeholder expectations of companies have changed; reporting is expected to be more than a compliance exercise.
     FRC solution: An objective-driven, communication-focused framework for all corporate reporting.
2   Corporate reporting is dispersed, containing fragmented and sometimes incoherent content.
     FRC solution: One common set of principles that apply across the system as a whole.
3   The annual report is serving multiple purposes and audiences.
     FRC solution: A reporting network structure to reflect multiple communication objectives.
4   The interests of investors have broadened, with the boundaries between shareholders and other stakeholders becoming increasingly blurred.
     FRC solution: A stakeholder-neutral approach to the identification of financial and non-financial corporate reporting content.
5   Technology has transformed how information is communicated, the annual report remains a paper-based document.
     FRC solution: Standardisation of non-financial reporting and the development of a Public Interest Report.

6   Non-financial reporting has evolved with multiple frameworks now
    guiding its form and content.
       FRC solution: Invite innovation for more dynamic production, dis-
    tribution and consumption of corporate reporting.

We will cover some of these aspects later in the book.

Notes

1 These refer to: Brydon Review, *Assess, assure and inform: improving audit
   quality and effectiveness* – final report of the independent review, December
   2019, available at: https://www.gov.uk/government/publications/the-quality-
   and-effectiveness-of-audit-independent-review, accessed December 2019.
      The Kingman Review and associated material is available at: https://www.gov.
   uk/government/news/independent-review-of-the-financial-reporting-council-
   frc-launches-report.
      The CMA Report and its associated material is available at: https://www.
   gov.uk/government/news/cma-recommends-shake-up-of-uk-audit-market,
   accessed December 2019.
2 It began in 2007 with a crisis in the subprime mortgage market in the US and
   developed into a full-blown international banking crisis, with the collapse of the
   investment bank Lehman Brothers on September 15, 2008. Excessive risk taking
   by banks such as Lehman Brothers helped to magnify the financial impact globally.
3 Who they still see receiving bonus payments to individuals of millions of
   pounds, over and above a very high basic salary and benefits.
4 FRC News, Audit firms implement 'additional measures' to enhance their evaluation of going concern assessments, *FRC*, 2 July 2020, available at: www.frc.
   org.uk/news/july-2020/audit-firms-implement-'additional-measures'-to-enh,
   accessed July 2020.
5 J. Hurley, Auditor admits 'significant doubt' over Pockit's future, *The Times*, 18
   July 2020, available at: www.thetimes.co.uk/article/auditor-admits-significant-
   doubt-over-pockits-future-8xb5p89tl, accessed July 2020.
6 N. Shepherd, 2019, Why audit changes will fail, *Economia*, 24 January 2019, available at: https://economia.icaew.com/opinion/january-2019/why-audit-changes-
   will-fail, accessed January 2019.
7 Michelin, G., Sealy, R., Trojanowski, G., Understanding research findings and
   evidence on corporate reporting: An independent literature review, *Commis-
   sioned by the FRC*, October 2020, available at: https://www.frc.org.uk/getat
   tachment/ba1c51d0-e933-4235-9c67-0bd2aa592edb/Literature-Review-Final.
   pdf, accessed October 2020.
8 ICAEW, What's next for corporate reporting: Time to decide? ICAEW website, 2017, page 3, available at: www.icaew.com/technical/financial-reporting/
   information-for-better-markets/what-next-for-corporate-reporting, accessed
   January 2018.
9 EY, EY center for board matters, 2018, available at: www.ey.com/Publica
   tion/vwLUAssets/ey-annual-reporting-in-2016-17-broad-perspective-clear-
   focus/%24FILE/EY-Annual-Reporting-in-2016-17.pdf, accessed January
   2018.

10 Victor Meldrew is a fictional character in the BBC One sitcom One Foot in the Grave.
11 FRC, The future of corporate reporting: A matter of principle, FRC Discussion paper, *FRC News*, 8 October 2020, available at: https://www.frc.org.uk/getattachment/cf85af97-4bd2-4780-a1ec-dc03b6b91fbf/Future-of-Corporate-Reporting-FINAL.pdf, accessed October 2020.
12 Brydon Review, Assess, assure and inform: Improving audit quality and effectiveness – final report of the independent review, December 2019, available at: www.gov.uk/government/publications/the-quality-and-effectiveness-of-audit-independent-review, accessed December 2019.
13 Kingman Report, Kingman report: Independent review of the financial reporting council, government, December 2018, available at: www.gov.uk/government/publications/financial-reporting-council-review-2018, accessed December 2018.
14 Op. Cit, FRC 2020 The future of corporate reporting discussion paper.

3 The investment industry

Failure of the present role of capital markets and financial reporting

Rules for financial reporting may or may not have worked before the pandemic of 2020. Our feeling is that they have failed. They exist, and they perform a function, but that function has changed. Post-pandemic, it is likely that they will change again. So this chapter deals with what we had and where we might be going. So possible functions that were important in the past but may be less relevant in the present circumstances (as mentioned earlier) include:

• Resource allocation: The classical function of financial reporting was to channel funds to the most productive business firms – for example, to facilitate the financing of new enterprises. This may have been the case in the 19th century but is not so relevant today. New entrants to the capital market are established medium-sized firms that seek a quotation to enable their founders to realise some part of their wealth.
• Distribution function of anticipated profits: This was a role taken on by financial reporting during the heyday of neo-liberalism, notably by the adoption of fair-value accounting. According to John Kay,[1] much of the profits reported with fair-value accounting were illusory and a major factor in the global financial crisis.

This may be too simplistic a view. Apart from debt financing (though we think this has declined until the onset of the pandemic), there are also a variety of seed, venture capital, semi-government, and crowdfunding initiatives, some of which are growing. These financing rounds often occur before a listing. They all require financial information, even though this money may have been invested with a mind to potential exit routes.

The professional investor uses financial reporting to a greater extent. Although some analysts we found rely on gut instinct, appraisal of management and informal discussions with management are often important. Later, we examine the evidence. But managed funds in the UK are currently greater than £2 trillion. For the US, this figure is greater than $25 trillion. For Europe, it is greater than €15 trillion (our estimates as of 2020). Some decisions to buy and sell are made by algorithmic programs that examine volume of trades, dark pools and price movements. Increasingly these are being augmented by intelligent systems, examining all market information, including messages from the company and any financial information (quarterly, annual, or profit updates). However, human analysis and thought still goes into a large chunk of trades and advice. Also, until recently, these professional investors made available their research and buy/sell decisions to all for free. This will still happen in the US, but MiFID (EU regulation) may limit this type of free service in the UK and Europe in future – depending on how far EU regulations are rolled back in 2021 (MiFID will probably be reduced in its UK influence).

Earlier, we posited that the function of financial reporting was no longer to guide the capitalist as to where he should invest his money (except where the investor is looking to move funds between individual shares or classes of investment) but rather to inform the capitalist how he could extract funds from the firm. However, with a plethora of new forms of funding, such as crowdfunding based on the internet, the traditional role of financial reporting may change.

If the role of financial reporting is not to aid the capitalist in making decisions about how much to invest in a business or how much to extract from a business, then what is its role? John Flower strongly believes that its role lies not in serving the capitalist or the capital markets but rather in serving the greater good of the whole of society. Corporate reporting can achieve this by concentrating on improving the wider accountability of the business firm. As financial reporting is the only vehicle through which a company is presently required to communicate to a large body (investors and other stakeholders), and that reporting is the only information that is audited, it is natural to extend financial reporting to encompass other desired corporate information even if it has minimal connection to financial reporting.

The vast majority of the people interviewed would say that the capital markets are not working at all well, but they do not want to see any major change – except perhaps a publicly funded bank to invest in industry. One argument is that the low-interest and easy-money regime following the GFC (starting from 2009) should have seen banks awash with money to lend to industry and businesses. Instead, and because of tighter rules, the banks, being in fear of lending money to anything that might be risky, lent money mainly for the purchase of property – leading to property price escalation.

Also, the role of raising new capital on the capital markets mainly goes to existing companies launching themselves on a stock market and the founders making a fortune as a result. Think of Facebook, Twitter, or Snapchat (Snap Inc.).

However, as we will discuss later, the presence of certain valuation rules (e.g. IAS39[2]) within financial reporting has a number of weaknesses. Many would hold that the deficiencies of fair-value accounting were a key cause of the weakness of banks, shown by the 2007 financial crisis. They only had to provide for actual incurred losses (rather than the possible predicted total loss) on loans no matter how certain the expected losses were. The same standard setters also required fair-value accounting in certain circumstances and have taken away prudence as an overriding concept. Both US and UK rules have been tightened since then.

The conventional wisdom of firms reporting to the shareholders who then invest or firms going to the shareholders to raise new finance has to be modified. Savers may use the stock market, but that often is not transferred to businesses as funding for new investment. So the concept that the investment industry plays a critical role in the economy, as the conduit through which money moves from savers to businesses, is essentially false.

As John Kay makes very clear in his book *Other People's Money*,[3] the stock exchange is not a source of investment money for business. New issues of shares are very rare; most new listings are ways for the founders of companies to realise their capital gains; the volume of share buybacks far exceeds the amount raised in new issues. Kay sums up the present position very well with the aphorism 'Stock markets are not a way of putting money into companies, but a means of taking it out'. That said, we have to qualify this in that the secondary AIM (Alternative Investment Market [sub-market of the London Stock Exchange]) market and venture capital do provide funding, though this is at the smaller end of the market. Also, new forms of financing are emerging, like crowdfunding (such as Kickstarter, Indiegogo, the much-advertised Funding Circle, and many more; to see more just 'Google' crowdfunding sites).

Supporting long-term investment and productivity requires effective dialogue between investors and companies. This refers to what Kay identified as the primary function of finance intermediaries (such as asset managers) now that the provision of new capital is less important. The primary function is to monitor the managers of companies to ensure that they are efficient and not self-serving.

Financing and investment industry and reporting function?

John Flower has a jaundiced view of the capital markets. They do not work. They are broken. They are a leech on society. They do not fulfil a worthy ethical function. In so far as reporting was primarily aimed at this sector, it should not; and it fulfils no purpose. Krish Bhaskar can see that the role of investors, analysts, and private equity firms has dramatically changed. And Rod Sellers, whilst acknowledging change, still feels that stock exchanges add value to society.

Now whatever one thinks of the stock exchanges and private equity firms and the financing/investment industry, their original role has changed. They do help people who have money increase their wealth. However, they are also a conduit for a large number of pensions used by companies, organisations, government, unions, universities, and other governmental or nongovernmental organisations. Such leveraged buyouts by private equity may have a solution from the US where the courts have ruled that creditors could go after a company's former directors if a private equity buyer saddles the business with an unsustainable amount of debt.

The demise of equity markets

There has been a trend to move from listed companies to taking them private to overcome the additional regulation that comes from the requirements of stock markets and reporting requirements. Also, shareholders can be annoying. Worse are the hedge funds, and those who wish to profit from options and changes in the price of shares can often influence management actions. Whitbread were more or less forced to sell Costa Coffee. Two activist shareholders, US hedge fund Elliott Advisors and Sachem Head, pressurised Whitbread's CEO (Chief Executive Officer), Alison Brittain. Short-seller Muddy Waters rightly (as it happens) continued to launch a bear attack on Burford Capital. (This was during 2019 and this led to Burford admitting illegal market manipulation and replacing its chief financial officer [CFO]). Hedge funds, short-sellers, and options traders can be (for management) a terrible nuisance and act as constraint on management of listed companies. But recently another reason has grown.

According to *The Economist*, the trend in the US has been:[4]

> America's stock of equity has been getting smaller for a while, because of share buy-backs, a secular fall in the number of new listings and the growing incidence of leveraged buy-outs, in which low-interest debt replaces equity. Britain is now the leading candidate for such 'de-equitisation', says Robert Buckland, of Citigroup. The net stock of equity outstanding has fallen by 3% since the start of 2018, faster than in America. Cheap debt is a factor. But debt is cheap everywhere. What makes Britain so ripe for the picking is its culture of accountability to shareholders. Activist investors, like Trian, can get results there.

The issue is a shift in the relative costs of debt and equity finance:[5]

> The prospective earnings yield on the FTSE All-Share index of London-listed stocks is 7.6%. Compare this with a proxy for an expected real return on corporate debt – the yield on investment-grade bonds less the current inflation rate, which is below zero. The gap between the two is the reward demanded for holding riskier stocks. It is also, by symmetry, a measure of the relative cost to companies of issuing equity versus debt.

This so called 'financing gap' is noticeably wide in Britain. It offers the scope to replace dear equity capital with cheap debt capital. *The Economist* argues:[6]

> The activist approach is to buy cheap-looking stocks and then work to get their latent value realised. This is more likely to succeed in Britain than in

Germany, Japan, South Korea or other places with cheap-looking cyclical stocks. It could involve a push to get a firm to buy back its own shares. It could mean hawking the company, or a division of it, to another company or to a private-equity firm. If buyers won't come to you, go to them by relisting somewhere that puts a higher value on your shares, such as America.

As yet there has been no backlash. Britain's stockmarket seems likely to shrink further. Whatever the means – under-the-radar buy-outs, mergers, spin-offs, or simply a drying-up of new issues – the underlying cause will be the same. Companies are turning their backs on the stockmarket because equity capital is relatively dear. The irony is that Britain's A-list shareholder culture makes its de-equitisation all the likelier.

Impact on financial reporting

In recent years with spare money, the growth of special purpose acquisition companies (SPAC) has emerged in 2020. Investors essentially write blank cheques to SPACs, which can take many months to target and buy another firm. At the moment it is difficult to list a SPAC in London, though this may change post-Brexit in 2021. As at the end of 2020 if you have a SPAC in the UK you have to suspend the shares at the point you announce a deal, and investors are then barred from trading again until the deal completes which could be several months. Post-Brexit SPACs could be encouraged in the UK.

With a diminishing number of listed firms, the impact on financial reporting is that the most stringent regulations (that is, for the public-interest entities, or PIEs) are being applied to fewer companies. That leaves a gap for those companies, some newly private, that are not listed and are owned by an increasing number of private equity companies or funds of one sort or another.

So one possibility and one that is ignored mostly by the regulatory authorities is to ensure that private-owned companies of sufficient size also have to comply with the same regulations, not so much to safeguard the shareholders, but more to comfort the wider set of stakeholders – those stakeholders becoming increasingly important in today's modern world.

Increasing burden of financial reporting on listed companies

One piece of evidence that is from the US and non-European markets is discussed below and shows that listed companies are responding to the tighter regulation of listed companies – that is, the separation of the CEO and chairman's job. This is not prevalent in the UK or Germany, where there are no examples of such a combined role in the FTSE 100 or DAX (in Germany). However, *The Economist* argued:[7]

It is not just scandal-prone firms that are choosing to split the two roles. Since 2001 the share of S&P 500 firms with one person tasked with both managing and governing has nearly halved. Britain's corporate-governance code frowns on the practice. Germany's bars it altogether. New regulations in America have made shareholders pay more attention to it. Likewise in Japan Inc.

The Economist makes the point that there is a popular belief that 'CEO duality' (combined role of CEO and chairman) allows for quicker execution of the board's strategic decisions and helps leadership maintain a unified front. And that is why non-listed firms, especially those companies run by founders, often adopt this approach. However, it can also dull a firm's checks and balances. *The Economist* points out that the resulting conflicts of interest may inflate executive salaries or discourage whistleblowing.[8]

Challenger, Gray & Christmas, a job placement firm, says that 2019 is on track for a record high turnover in the corner office. Since September [2019] heads have rolled at WeWork, eBay and SAP. If trends hold, newly minted bosses should not expect to oversee themselves.

Merger, takeover, and acquisition environment

Debenhams collapse (2020) in our view stemmed from a short spell of private equity ownership that enriched its backers with £1.2 billion in dividends but starved the department store of investment required to survive. Moreover, they financed the deal with more than £1 billion of debt and went on to engineer sale and leasebacks that raised half a billion pounds and trapped the department store with 35-year-long rent agreements. Sir Philip Green's Arcadia's collapsed in the same year The entrepreneur bought Arcadia in 2002 with borrowed money, cut costs and refinanced the business that paid his Monaco-based wife (the ultimate legal owner) a £1.2 billion dividend in 2005. This habit of loading a company with debt and then repaying the purchase amount and taking (what may be regarded as) excessive dividends is a hallmark of private equity and entrepreneurial-owned companies.

As we go to print, the current economic environment has seen a fluctuating level of mergers, acquisitions, and takeover bids, often involving hedge funds, other short sellers, vulture funds, and asset strippers and also due to the genuine desire to become stronger whilst profits are being made. The period of 2017 to 2020, we think, will see all-time records in the value of mergers and acquisitions. This activity raises its own problems – the merged firms suddenly find that their accounting rules and valuation methods do not match. Moreover, as with Autonomy Corporation,[9] the company taking over another may find that the price they paid was made on what they regard as massively different valuations and underlying assumptions.

In the US, as one might expect, the number of lawsuits that emanate from the results of a takeover or merger is on the increase. Class-action lawsuits centralise a number of claims into one venue in which a court can equitably divide the assets amongst all the plaintiffs if they win the case. Sometimes a class action of shareholders is sponsored by a private equity company or a hedge fund with the drumming up of support from a wider grouping of shareholders.[10]

Cornerstone Research produces an annual report,[11] which shows the number of class-action lawsuits filed in the US. The number of accounting-related filings reached a record number of 165 during 2017, nearly twice the 88 filed the previous year. The overall increase in accounting case filings was mainly attributable to 107 filings related to mergers and acquisitions.

All of them contained accounting disclosure allegations. Of course, the lawsuits can be hedge funds and private equity companies, who may also be shareholders of the company being taken over or the company acquiring. Either set of shareholders might feel hard done by. Then as with Autonomy, it can also be the management. The issue is always disclosures, valuations, and the accounting rules that make up the balance sheet and income figures. Then when the merged group produces new consolidated accounts, there may be large intangible assets with a large goodwill sum for the purchase of the company taken over. If overvalued this can create more and new problems.

MiFID I and II

The EU's regulatory reforms, known as MiFID I & II (Markets in Financial Instruments Directive), have transformed Europe's financial industry. In theory, it is designed to offer greater protection for investors and inject more transparency into all asset classes, from equities to fixed income, exchange traded funds and foreign exchange – including options, derivatives, and other financial instruments. The extensive piece of legislation took seven years to prepare and already has more than 1.4 million paragraphs of rules, which will continue to grow. Though this piece of EU regulations is likely to be trimmed in the new 2021 Brexit rules.

Again in theory, the directive seeks to open up opaque markets by forcing brokers and trading venues to report prices publicly and in close to real time for those assets deemed liquid. Also, these rules require markets to report to regulators up to 65 separate data points on every trade – with the aim of avoiding market abuse. The changes are greatest for markets dealing in bonds and derivatives that are now largely conducted 'over the counter' and not on exchanges. But the directive also

a   Restricts share trading in 'dark pools' (commonest in the US) that are closed to retail investors
b   Provides access to European markets for non-EU firms
c   Requires investment banks to start charging separately for research, among a myriad of other provisions.

Pre-MFiD investment analysts used to send their views and analysis of companies to potential shareholders and investors free-of-charge as a service. Now they have to charge. But hedge funds and other short sellers have taken their place. (Short selling occurs when an investor borrows a security and sells it on the open market, planning to buy it back later for less money. Short sellers bet on, and profit from, a drop in a security's price.) Sometimes the same investors issue a report of why the share value should fall which aids that very fall. If fully implemented, it is perhaps the biggest regulatory change to European financial markets since the financial crisis. But it may place the EU at a substantial disadvantage to the UK and New York. This directive could hasten the centralisation of banking on New York and to banking becoming smaller in the EU.

Our view is that with the UK leaving the EU, probably the full provisions of MiFID II will never be implemented, though they may remain on the statute book. The European Securities and Markets Authority (ESMA) and the EU regulator has already granted some reprieve and given the big exchanges a delay until after 2020 or beyond, when the UK will have officially left the EU and will be charting new 'just UK' rules.

Notes

1 See John Kay, *Other People's Money: Masters of the Universe or Servants of the People?* Profile Books, 2016, p. 130 ff.
2 IAS 39 is an international accounting standard dealing with financial instruments: Recognition and Measurement is an international accounting standard for financial instruments released by the International Accounting Standards Board (IASB). It was replaced in 2014 by IFRS 9, which becomes effective in 2018. It was adopted by the EU in 2004.
3 Pages 160–164.
4 Buttonwood, Britain's equity market is shrinking, *Economist*, 17 October 2019, available at: www.economist.com/finance-and-economics/2019/10/17/britains-equity-market-is-shrinking, accessed October 2019.
5 Ibid.
6 Ibid.
7 *Economist*, Power decouples: CEO-chairmen are an endangered species, *Economist*, 17 October 2019, available at: www.economist.com/business/2019/10/17/ceo-chairmen-are-an-endangered-species, accessed October 2019.
8 Though studies examining the link between company performance and CEO-chairmanships have been collectively inconclusive.
9 K. Bhaskar et al., *Financial Failures & Scandals: From Enron to Carillion*, Vol. 2, Routledge, 2019, available at: www.amazon.co.uk/Financial-Failures-Scandals-Carillion-Disruptions-ebook/dp/B07QTB4DJ6.
   Also: www.fin-rep.org/buy/
10 This is the case in a lawsuit brought against Macquarie Infrastructure Corporation for a drop in its share value of 41%.
   See J. Kehoe, Macquarie infrastructure Corp faces class action lawsuits, *Financial Review*, 2 May 2018, available at: www.afr.com/business/macquarie-infrastructure-corp-faces-class-action-lawsuits-20180501-h0zilt, accessed July 2018.
11 M. Cohn, 2018, Accounting class-action suits hit record levels, *Accounting Today*, 18 April 2018, available at: www.accountingtoday.com/news/accounting-class-action-lawsuits-hit-record-levels, accessed July 2018.

4 The current reporting and auditing environment

The financial reporting backcloth

Since most of our readers will be familiar with much of this material, the fuller version of this chapter is provided in Appendix 3.04.1. This omits many items that the well-versed reader already knows. Once again, financial reporting and corporate reporting will no doubt have fundamental changes. Pre-pandemic, environmental concerns were taking shape, but post-pandemic there will be other concerns – perhaps focusing on survival?

The pace of change

This has been and will continue to be hectic. Starting with the crisis facing Carillion and its collapse, there is a timeline which leads up to the CMA review, the Kingman review, the Brydon review, and then other recent failures (such as Patisserie Valerie and Thomas Cook; in total, about 40 cases[1]), which resulted in a fundamental reappraisal of reporting and auditing. A detailed description is given in Appendix 3.04.1.

Disruption in reporting timeline

Basically the newly beefed-up FRC/ARGA wants the breakup of the Big Four. That and with many other changes to financial reporting, the standards and the auditing requirements have been laid out and are changing consciously as a reaction to the many failures. The accounting standards are also continually being revised.

Pandemic special issues

The Economist[2] highlighted threats to going back to normal. The first was follow-up waves of infection. The second concerns the political backcloth, as the effects of the ensuing recession would hit workers and small firms to a greater extent. The second threat concerns us more directly, and *The Economist* reckons that the pandemic recession will expose accounting wrongdoing and frauds.

> A second hazard to reckon with is fraud. Extended booms tend to encourage shifty behaviour, and the expansion before the covid crash was the longest on record. Years of cheap money and financial engineering mean that accounting shenanigans may now be laid bare. Already there have been two notable scandals in Asia in recent weeks, at Luckin Coffee, a Chinese Starbucks wannabe, and Hin Leong, a Singaporean energy trader that has been hiding giant losses. A big fraud or corporate collapse in America could rock the markets' confidence, much as the demise of Enron shredded investors' nerves in 2001 and Lehman Brothers led the stockmarket down in 2008.

The two cases mentioned in the above article are discussed in: www.fin-rep. org.

Both of these are clear cases of deliberately falsifying accounts and will lead to court cases. The UK is not alone, and in our site above, we have more than 100 such cases of accounting errors found in UK companies (deliberate or not – spreadsheet errors being one cause of non-deliberate errors).

The FT[3] also opined the same:

> The reputation of Britain's accountancy firms has been damaged in recent years by a string of corporate collapses they didn't see coming. Now auditors say that they have been thrown into the most challenging working environment of their careers as they attempt to spot potential fraud and calculate the likelihood of businesses surviving the crisis – all while in lockdown and under increased regulatory scrutiny.
>
> 'The risks are not different from those you would normally find as an auditor but the risk is turbo-heightened and more pronounced than it's ever been around going concern', said Stephen Griggs, 55, who is overseeing Deloitte's audit work in 27 countries from his kitchen.

So expect a few more accounting errors and fraud to crop up postpandemic crisis. Especially during the crisis, the risk of fraud is heightened. Directors could be tempted to tweak accounts to improve their chances of survival. Auditors also have to be wary of directors using the crisis to try to flush out bad news on their balance sheets by falsely attributing it to COVID-19. And this applies as much in the front end as the back end of the annual report. Not being able to make site visits to watch stock counts, review documents, and attend board meetings increases the risk of fraud.

Audit fees: we expect the Big Four and other audit firms to dramatically increase their audit fees for 'so-called' additional costs during the pandemic. We have seen evidence of such rises which could not be entirely justified by such increased costs. Though we feel that audit fees up to now have been in general too low.

The major players in reporting

The chief executive, the board, its committees, particularly the audit committee, the NEDs (non-executive directors), and the shareholders are all major players. However, the other stakeholders (suppliers, customers, community and government) are becoming more important than hitherto.

In theory, shareholders hold the absolute power, but in practice, they choose not to exercise it. Shareholders came in for their own criticism from the Carillion joint select committees: 'Big shareholders were not inquisitive'.[4] Even when there is a dispute, the board usually has the proxy votes from the big institutional shareholders, and so they usually win (99% of the time in Krish Bhaskar's subjective view).

However, every now and again, the shareholders do have a revolt – usually about excessive pay awards for the board. Remuneration committees select consultants to help them judge appropriate pay awards and overall remuneration. It is a cosy club, and it seems these awards always spiral upwards regardless of economic conditions or actual company performance.

There are some share action groups (proxy advisers), including Share Action, ISS, PIRC, and Glass Lewis, which can help to mobilise the power of shareholders. In general, unless there are institutional shareholders with a large stake, they are more or less ignored and powerless. That may change with the forthcoming new governance code.

The House of Commons Parliamentary select committee

As we have seen, of all the watchdogs, the new parliamentary phenomenon has proved the most influential. They do not pull their punches. They are now fast and hard-hitting but try to ascertain the facts and do not suffer fools gladly.

The chairs of (the majority of) select committees have been elected by the house as a whole since June 2010, and that has made them much more efficient

Reports: the annual report

Up to now, we have been referring to financial and corporate reports as if they were a fixed items. They are not. They are a living organism which is constantly evolving and changing. Many would view the annual report as the principal company report. We make these distinctions in this book and its appendices: hard, soft, strategic, sustainable, non-financial, forward-looking, and hybrid; and one that might not be immediately obvious: entropic (think informational content). The US has much less soft information that is mandatory. The UK probably has more than any other country in the EU.

The current report requirements are constantly being added, based partly on FRC regulations and partly on statutory instruments from Parliament.

Financial statement components

Increasingly, the annual report might be split into a number of reports. Sometimes these are named:

Strategic report
Transparency report
Sustainability report

The annual report has its own set of standards under the voluntary Global Reporting Initiative (GRI).[5] The GRI is an international independent standards organisation that helps businesses, governments, and other organisations understand and communicate their impacts on issues such as climate change, human rights, and corruption.

The regulators and watchdogs

These are the policemen, judges, and jury in the financial world. Our main concern in this book is with the top two regulators, FRC and ARGA – the second one (ARGA) might replace the FRC. Or there may be a stronger, more proactive FRC. But there will not be both.

In summary, we have the following watchdogs now in the UK:

FRC/ARGA – annual reports and auditing
FCA – Financial Conduct Authority for listed companies and markets
TPR – The Pensions Regulator

The Equality and Human Rights Commission – gender pay gap
PRA – Prudential Regulation Authority for banks and lenders
Department for Business, Energy & Industrial Strategy (BEIS) – payments practices and directors' conduct
Insolvency Service – may get enhanced powers to pursue directors, currently takes to court around 1,200 directors
SFO – Serious Fraud Office pursuing cases where there is a possibility of fraud, but its reputation is that it takes too long (e.g. Tesco case) and that its conviction rate is too low. Though they seem to keep on failing, the latest is with Barclays Bank on their Qatari funding which might have been a round-trip type of possibly illegal manoeuvre – no criminal case proven but civil cases from associated parties continue.
Select committees – all areas, fast and hard hitting but with no power or teeth.

When presented like this, we think this is too fragmented and split between too many agencies. And we agree that there are insufficient sanctions against management of the companies making inaccurate, false, or misleading reports – as already noted the government seems to be tightening regulations. Company regulations may increase markedly if all the various recent reviews are implemented though it will take some time to be placed on the statute book.

The narrative section

The sections in the annual report have been divided into hard (numbers) and soft (mainly words and/or analysis of numbers). The narrative section includes such elements as:

Strategic (soft)
Viability (over 12 months)/Going-concern (up to 12 months) [soft-ish]
Forward-looking/Resilience (Brydon) [soft but may include some hard information]
Sustainable (soft)
Non-financial (tends to be soft but with some numbers)

This is further discussed in Appendix 3.04.1.

Interim statements

In the same appendix, the importance of quarterly and half-yearly reports is argued. The danger is that it induces myopic management behaviour.[6]

New types of information

There is a range of new types of information being required by UK companies. Some of these are UK specific and go further than the EU rules. Most of these are unlikely to be rolled back in a low regulation environment post-Brexit. They are here to stay either because companies have become used to these measures or they have become industry specific or market demanded as standard. More rules and regulations will come. Although there may be some easing back by the low regulation of the Boris Johnson government.

APMs (Alternative Performance Measures) are financial oriented, whilst KPIs (Key Performance Indicators) tend to be volume or quantity or percentage oriented – such as occupancy rates and so on.

Companies from 2016 are required to publish an annual slavery and trafficking statement in a prominent place on their website.[7] We have not found much evidence that firms are actually complying with the spirit of this regulations. Some are. In general, it is a boilerplate response. And we see no reason to suspect that this will change even in a low-regulation post-Brexit environment.

From 2017, the government published new regulations implementing the EU Directive on disclosure of non-financial and diversity information (the Non-Financial Reporting Directive). The regulations amend the Companies Act 2006 requirements for the Strategic Report and include diversity requirements in the Disclosure and Transparency Rules (DTR). We suspect that will continue whether we move to a low regulation environment or not.

Government BEIS website reporting

Gender pay gap and supplier payment information is now mandatory. See Appendix 3.04.5 'New methods of reporting' for further details. This is likely to be the trend with self-reporting under guidelines as to non-financial information and/or policy. Now that we are in a possibly low-regularity environment, nothing may be added for some time. But there are other measures such as 'How good is it to work in your company?' as per *The Sunday Times* survey.[8]

Climate change disclosures

In the world of climate change and following the development of integrated reporting (now nearly defunct in our view), the watchdogs themselves will push for greater disclosures. Hence, UK-listed companies will face greater and often compulsory disclosures on climate change over the next few years.

Initially and surprisingly, it is the FCA (Financial Conduct Authority) which is reported to be bringing forward proposals to help investors and support the transition to a low carbon economy[9]: Under these proposals all companies that have their main listing in London must make climate-related disclosures as prescribed by the Financial Stability Board's Taskforce [TCFD]) on Climate-related Financial Disclosures – or explain why they cannot.[10]

Annual reporting: CORE/MORE = hybrid

Investors and other stakeholders often have much in common, and on some issues information primarily of interest to other stakeholders will also be material to investors and should be reported to them. But if an annual report focused on investors is to remain the cornerstone of the corporate reporting process, what of the information needs of other stakeholders? The Federation of European Accountants (FEE) published an influential report[11] suggesting a CORE and MORE approach for corporate reporting. We build on that seminal report.

So we postulate a hybrid system (several parallel reports) with a core report and then, emanating from and consistent with that core, a number of more detailed reports geared to the needs of each type of user or stakeholder. This is also more likely to require self-service for those classes of users catered for. This hybrid reporting system is in sharp contrast to 'integrated reporting', in which there is a single all-encompassing report. There is a growing need not to put everything in one report. A summary of the remuneration report on one or two pages could then link to the detailed report, which may run into 20 or more pages.

Several senior partners at the Big Four, when confronted with the concept, felt that a hybrid system could well be the right way for companies to experiment with a new style of reporting. One said in an interview:

> And I think the increments should be added depending on the needs of the stakeholders in that particular company. So, the hybrid reporting might evolve differently for different companies.

The need for hybrid reporting emanated from ever-expanding annual reports. For example, the HSBC Annual Report of 2014 had grown to 598 pages (322 pages in 2018); RBS's Annual Report at the end of 2013 was 564 pages (267 pages in 2018). In both cases, much is unintelligible to anyone not trained in (a) accounting and finance or (b) as a banker and (c) specific jargon relating to HSBC or RBS. All three of the authors, all of whom are skilled at reading annual reports and financial statements, including those of banks, found many pages in both reports difficult to read and understand.

Hence the set of annual or quarterly information is sometimes, and may increasingly be, contained within a number of distinct reports; and these reports may combine several different elements.

Distribution function

In his book on accounting and distributive justice,[12] John Flower makes the strong argument about how the distribution function for stakeholders should dominate the reporting and information function (some may see this as a philosophical distinction). This also set out John's view on the need for different reports to satisfy different functions and differing sets of users.

Hence hybrid reporting

Investors and other stakeholders often have much in common, and on some issues information primarily of interest to other stakeholders will also be material to investors and should be reported to them. But if an annual report focused on investors is to remain the cornerstone of the corporate reporting process, what of the information needs of other stakeholders? A number of themes have emerged here, summarised in what follows.

Though several senior partners at the Big Four, when confronted with the concept, felt that a hybrid system could well be the right way for companies to experiment with a new style of reporting. One said in an interview:

> And I think the increments should be added depending on the needs of the stakeholders in that particular company. So, the hybrid reporting might evolve differently for different companies.

Box 4.1   Hybrid Reporting covers:

External	CORE & MORE reports
	Standard reports for stakeholders
	Tailored reports for different classes of stakeholders
	Self-service reports for stakeholders with suitable privileges
	CORE & MORE for shareholders
	CORE & MORE for professional investors
	CORE & MORE reports for employees
Internal	CORE & MORE for different classes of management and employees

---

Self-service reports for internal stakeholders with suitable privileges e.g. employees
Management standard reports
Self-service reports for management with suitable permissions
Self-service reports for employees with suitable permissions
Operational standard reports
Self-service reports for operations

It won't give a perfect answer straight away – but neither will any of the other solutions. The hybrid solution will give a company a relatively low-cost/low-risk way of starting to make change. Companies will look at what others are doing, and the next year's reporting will reflect what they have learnt. The full plethora of reports under Hybrid is shown in Box 4.1. The CORE and MORE is extended by tailored and self-service reports allowed by direct access to the raw or semi-structured data.

The FRC Reporting multiple report network[13]

The FRC proposals involve a network of multiple reports. The CORE reports would be:

–   the Business Report
–   the full Financial Statements
–   and a new Public Interest Report (not just for PIEs).

The Business Report would provide information that enables users to understand how the company creates long-term value in accordance with its stated purpose. The FRC envisages this being similar to a concise Strategic Report, including financial and non-financial information.

These reports would address the most important objectives in the communication between companies and their stakeholders. There would be another series of unbundled reports. These network (MORE) reports would be accessible and could be a mixture and mandatory and voluntary reports:

•   Supporting detail – provides additional detail on information contained in the Business Report such as divisional performance.
•   Special purpose report – provide information that is for a specific purpose such as investor presentations.

- Standing data – is a location for a master file of data which does not frequently change such as policy information.
- Other reports – for additional periodic reports provided at a different time frame such as half-year reports.

The FRC proposes that there should be one set of principles.

a) System level attributes: the qualitative characteristics that reporting, as a whole, should possess. These include: accessibility, consistency, connectivity (interconnected series of multiple reports), and transparency.
b) Report level attributes: the qualitative characteristics that an individual report should possess. This includes both the twin tests of fair balanced and understandable (something we find has not worked well) and the true and fair test (as per the Companies Act 2006).
c) Content communication principles: the principles of effective communication, applied when preparing an individual report. This includes brevity, comprehensibility, and usefulness relevance, company specific information, and comparability.

In a subsequent online presentation the FRC's Deepa Raval examined proportionality by saying that size would determine which reports could be provided:

Small/micro entities:	Financial Statements
Medium & Large:	Financial Statements + Business Report
PIEs:	Financial Statements + Business Report + Public Interest Report

All three size tiers of companies would produce supporting detail, special purpose report, standing data, and 'other reports'. This, we think, is a pity. All companies of any size (listed and private) should produce the Business Report (even Arcadia's short business reports in their Annual Reports), were small but highly relevant – until very recently before the company's collapse). Size and number of sections and detail could provide the proportionality not the absence of information.

However we have other major concerns which are discussed in Chapter 8.

More frequent communications between company and the public

The annual report is the main corporate report for many readers, but there are other equally important communications (as judged by our and other empirical evidence). As one senior partner of the Big Four proclaimed:

> The other observation I have about today's corporate reporting is that whilst the 'official' annual report & accounts is released annually, companies actually communicate with their stakeholders much more frequently, almost on a real-time basis. This means that the weighty, complex and retrospective set of historical financial statements is at risk of becoming irrelevant.

Of course, meetings with executives are not public, so those executives have to be careful of breaking market rules and of creating a situation which might be deemed to be insider trading. That said, management seemed to be blissfully unconcerned about privileged information leaking out. We found much evidence that it did leak – but not for anything major such as a merger or takeover bid or a major profits warning.

The empirical work undertaken by EY[14] shows that active professional investors use different information depending on where they are in their purchase of shares or their own investment cycle.

> Our research has shown us that the value placed by investors on different sources of information varies with the stage in the investment cycle. From a small sample of investors we surveyed separately within investment institutions and conversations we have had with some others, it seems that for portfolio managers and others involved in the investment decision, the annual report is a primary source of research material when making a first time investment decision – although used alongside analyst presentations and meetings with executives, which are also ranked highly.
>
> Once the initial investment has been made, annual reports, although remaining important, lose prominence. Meetings with executives become the primary source of information, while analyst presentations and preliminary announcements gain importance. As might be expected, the smaller the investor and the less the resource available, the more likely they are to rely on third parties for analysis and recommendations.

EY feel that this should not undermine the importance of annual reports. They go on to say:

> Although share prices are perceived to move more on preliminary announcements, this simply reflects that they are the first insight into the company's performance, not the best. Rather, within a wider set

of sources used by a range of stakeholders, annual reports retain primacy. They are the most read and disseminated document, are assured, are more detailed and holistic, and are the only source for many kinds of information (e.g., governance, business model and risks). The main challenge for companies is to ensure the consistency and balance of messaging across all corporate communications, especially as boards are required to present a fair, balanced, and understandable assessment of the company's position and prospects in not only the annual report, but also interim and other price-sensitive reports.[15]

Analysts' presentations versus meetings with executives

EY put some store into preliminary announcements. See Box 4.2. We could not duplicate their findings in all the interviews and evidence we collected. On the other hand, we found that analysts' presentations had much greater importance. However, EY found that meetings with executives become of greater importance for active professional investors. Our evidence confirmed this. Although this was certainly mentioned in our interviews, it was not something that interviewees drew a lot of attention to – maybe afraid of being tainted with an implication of receiving privileged information ahead of the market? But more likely, they did not wholly believe the information that was given to them – believing it to be filtered and biased in some way. But we believe that the EY conclusions are correct – for active professional investors. Meetings with executives would not occur with a wider set of smaller investors or other stakeholders (except perhaps for those few shareholders who choose to attend an AGM [annual general meeting]).

Box 4.2   Selected EY Comments on Analysts' Presentations[16]

All companies we reviewed publish their presentations for analysts and investors on their websites.

The vast majority of analyst presentations contain disclosures on strategy and priorities for the future, but only half articulate the company's strategy in a way consistent with the annual report – and sometimes this information isn't clearly labelled as the company's strategy (with other priorities getting more prominence). Conversely, a few companies provide clearer narrative and graphics to articulate their strategy in their analysts' presentations than in their annual report.

A significant proportion of analyst presentations convey messages that are inconsistent with those disclosed in the annual report.

Some presentations focus on different aspects of the company's activities to those highlighted most prominently in the annual report, while others portray a more positive and less balanced picture.

Profit warnings

A profit warning is more formal. It is a warning or declaration issued by a listed company to investors and shareholders. It warns investors that the profit of the company in the coming quarter/half-year/year will significantly decline when compared with market expectations and analysts' predictions. Sometimes it is a guide for analysts to reduce their expectations of profitability. Meeting analysts becomes important. Usually, the company will try to massage analysts' expectations during the year towards a realistic outcome. This massaging takes place through analysts' meetings.

A typical profits warning is like this:

> Banknote maker De La Rue sees shares tumble 13% after profit warning as shown by:[17]
>
> De La Rue, the maker of the new polymer £5 and £10 notes, issued a profit warning today and revealed the departure of its finance chief in an unscheduled announcement. The unexpected news sent shares in the company down more than 13 per cent or 82p lower to 520p.
>
> De La Rue said it was expecting its full-year results to be around the lower end of the current consensus range, but did not say why. Consensus estimates for operating profit currently sit in the range of £69 million to £73 million.

One has to read between the lines. The CFO (Chief Financial Officer) was leaving. Perhaps there was something untoward? Perhaps not. Perhaps the company knew that they were unlikely to win the new Brexit passport contract, but the suspicion will be there. And why warn that the profits estimates would be towards the bottom end of a range when that is quite normal – £69 million instead of £73 million is not really a significant amount.

Then in April, there was a second profits warning, with the company downgrading its expected underlying operating profit for the year to about £60 million – and this was after the decision on the passport contract went to a rival of De La Rue. The company's share price tumbled. But profits came in slightly higher than the warning £63 million.

Worse was to follow. Two profit warnings were made in 2019, and the second of which wiped out more than a fifth off the value of De La Rue. This setback follows the high profile loss of the contract to print British passports to a French company in 2018. In July 2019 the SFO opened an investigation into the group over suspected corruption in South Sudan, while, in May 2019, De La Rue revealed an £18 million shortfall after the Venezuelan central bank failed to pay its bills. De La Rue then warned on Thursday that full-year profits would be significantly lower than expectation and that profits would be hit by heightened competition.

The company brought in a new chairman and CEO in an attempt to rectify the situation. That said, De La Rue's share price has fallen four-fifths since the start of 2018 to a 21-year low, and dropped 20% to 150 pence – recovered somewhat in 2020 to a high of just below 170 pence. Analysts believe that the new top management can draw a line under the past and move forward.[18]

Increasing divergence between book and market values (the intangibles problem)

There is an increasing divergence between book values and market values. This might be partially attributed to information (often non-financial) that is outside of the financial report – such as the number of online users. Some of this gap is attributed to non-financial information within the report itself. However, as there is no clarity as to what external information is a driver of value, there may be considerable differences between industry sectors. Deloitte[19] and others rightly say there is also a lot of noise, which may result in the information being visible only to those with the tools and skills to cut through the fog. Sometimes that information is available to a privileged few, as shown by the numerous presentations to analysts/media.

Now the stock market value of a firm and its actual performance bear little resemblance to any valuation formula that we have traditionally been taught, such as multiples of profits or the net present value of a dividend stream. Market values can be just sky high. Companies which make a loss can still be valued in billions. Snap Inc (the chat app Snapchat) has a market capitalisation of around $25 billion, down from $30 billion on its initial day of trading in March 2017. Yet during the full year 2017, Snap Inc reported a net loss of $3.4 billion, up from $0.5 billion the previous year. And its net free cash outflow was close to $1 billion (negative cash flow). But daily active users increased by 18% year over year to 187 million. Investors obviously equate that figure to represent future revenue streams through advertising. This has not changed for Snap Inc. In 2019 the company reported a loss of over $1 billion on revenues of $1.7 billion, and its market capitalisation was approaching $80 billion by the end of 2020. We will go into this further in Chapter 9 with some solutions. See also Appendix 3.04.13 (A note on intangibles).

Big data

As discussed more fully in Chapter 6, another big driver could be big data, which includes social media and the chat apps. These can influence the purchase decision. Tripadvisor has become mandatory whether you believe the reviews or not. Interviewees report that they have seen how they can strike fear into the heart of a small hotel owner, who will often bend over backwards to avoid a negative report. Conversely, the sheer volume is important and has lead Edgar House in Chester (UK) to be voted the most romantic hotel in the world.(Tripadvisor 2017 survey), with 589 reviews for a seven-bedroom boutique hotel![20]

Forward-looking statements

There is an increasing focus on non-financial information and a growing requirement to provide forward-looking information including essentially a numerical forecast of the business and additional 'what if' questions answered. This is an area that we believe will be expanded.

Of course, forward-looking statements can be

1   Based just on financial statements with or without numerical values
2   Using non-financial information and metrics such as volumes, with or without numerical values
3   Providing a view of the competitive environment and competitive information and the impact on the company in question.

Items 2 and 3 could include units, pricing, segmentation, market share, and market penetration, and this can be provided with multiple scenarios, with sensitivity analyses and stress tests.

As we noted before, there is growing interest in including forward-looking information and indicators. A recent survey by KPMG, the Survey of Business Reporting, reported that 25% of the companies included (270 companies across 16 countries) provide short-term forecasts in their annual reports.[21]

This suggests a way of improving the value relevance of the annual report and adds to the debate on the purpose of the annual report and whether its role is primarily confirmatory or predictive. We think it will move towards being more predictive.

The Brydon review breaks the future down into three reports:[22]

> The future can be broken down into different time periods about which the directors should be able to make statements with varying degrees of confidence: the short term (up to two years), the medium term (from the end of the short term to five years) and the long term (beyond five years), an indeterminate period. It would better inform users of financial statements if these three time periods were brought together in a coherent view of the future, linked firmly to the directors' Risk Report.

Each of these time periods has its own test and definition, including survival, and different scenarios and possible longer-term threats. And of course stress testing. The auditors would need to report to the FRC/ARGA if there is any weakness or anxiety about the resilience in all three time periods. We also think that it may be useful to prepare forecasts for a fan of potential outcomes as used by the Bank of England (called fan charts).

Integrated reporting

Integrated reporting was a good start to expanding the scope of reporting. However, whilst still keeping to some of its original ideals, we argue that it seems to have not fully succeeded in its current form. One author believes that this movement has failed. This book adds to integrated reporting with a thoroughly practical form of financial reporting – hybrid accounting – which should enable accounting and financial reporting to meet the challenge of the future. It relies heavily on new technology and being clear and concise.

Notes

1 See our site (updated regularly): www.fin-rep.org/which-book/financial-failures-scandals-from-enron-to-carillion/post-publication-discussion/.
2 Leader, A dangerous gap: The market v the real economy, *Economist*, 7 May 2020, available at: www.economist.com/leaders/2020/05/07/the-market-v-the-real-economy, accessed: May 2020.

3 L. Clarence-Smith, Auditors face biggest challenge yet with reputation on the line, *The Times*, 13 May 2020, available at: www.thetimes.co.uk/article/auditors-face-biggest-challenge-yet-with-reputation-on-the-line-v882jtswk, accessed: May 2020.

4 N. Pratley, Entire system failed Carillion, not just directors at the top, *The Guardian*, 16 May 2018, available at: www.theguardian.com/business/nils-pratley-on-finance/2018/may/16/entire-system-failed-carillion-not-just-directors-at-the-top, accessed May 2020.

5 See the GRI website: www.globalreporting.org/Pages/default.aspx, accessed May 2020.

6 The FRC has launched a consultation on the proposed revision of its review standard for interim financial statements in December 2020. https://www.frc.org.uk/news/november-2020/consultation-on-revised-review-standard-(isre-(uk)

7 Statutory guidance: Slavery and human trafficking in supply chains: Guidance for businesses, UK Government, 20 April 2020, available at: www.gov.uk/government/publications/transparency-in-supply-chains-a-practical-guide, accessed May 2020.

   See who is required to comply? in Transparency in Supply Chains etc. A practical guide. A Home Office publication, Guidance issued under section 54(9) of the Modern Slavery Act 2015, available at: https://assets.publishing.service.gov.uk/government/uploads/system/uploads/attachment_data/file/649906/Transparency_in_Supply_Chains_A_Practical_Guide_2017.pdf, accessed October 2019.

8 Available at: www.b.co.uk/the-lists/

9 T. Kinder, UK-listed companies face compulsory climate disclosures, *Financial Times*, available at: www.ft.com/content/de915fb4-5f9e-11ea-b0ab-339c2307bcd4, accessed March 2020.

10 FCA, FCA announces proposals to improve climate-related disclosures by listed companies, 6 March 2020, available at: www.fca.org.uk/news/press-releases/fca-announces-proposals-improve-climate-related-disclosures-listed-companies, accessed March 2020.

11 The Federation of European Accountants, The future of corporate reporting – Creating the dynamics for change, Cogito series, October 2015, available at: www.accountancyeurope.eu/wp-content/uploads/FEECogitoPaper_-_Futureof CorporateReporting.pdf, accessed March 2020.

12 J. Flower, *Accounting and Distributive Justice*, Routledge 2010.

13 FRC, The future of corporate reporting discussion paper, *FRC News*, 8 October 2020, available at: https://www.frc.org.uk/news/october-2020/frc-publishes-future-of-corporate-reporting-discus, accessed October 2020.

14 EY Annual Reporting in 2017/17: Broad perspective, clear focus, September 2017, available at: www.ey.com/Publication/vwLUAssets/EY_-_Annual_Reporting_in_2016-17/$FILE/ey-annual-reporting-in-2016-17.pdf, accessed December 2019.

15 EY is your non-financial performance revealing the true value of your business to investors? 2017, available at: www.ey.com/Publication/vwLUAssets/EY_-_Nonfinancial_performance_may_influence_investors/$FILE/ey-nonfinancial-performance-may-influence-investors.pdf, accessed December 2019.

16 EY, Center for board matters, 2019, available at: www.ey.com/uk/en/issues/governance-and-reporting/corporate-governance/ey-annual-reporting-in-2016-17-broad-perspective-clear-focus, accessed December 2019.

17 'This is Money' on 20 March 2018.
18 Thomas, D., and McCormick, M., De La Rue shares tumble 20% after second profit warning this year, *Financial Times*, 30 October 2019. Available at: https://www.ft.com/content/6c6aa20c-fae4-11e9-a354-36acbbb0d9b6
    See also https://www.delarue.com/investors/results-reports-and-presentations/latest-results https://www.ft.com/content/29aff78c-634b-11e8-a39d-4df188287fff, accessed December 2019.
19 'Thinking allowed – The future of corporate reporting', July 2016, Deloitte.
20 C. Riches, This hotel has beaten rivals in Paris, Venice and Barcelona to be crowned the most romantic in Europe, *Daily Mirror*, 30 January 2017, available at: www.mirror.co.uk/news/uk-news/hotel-beaten-rivals-paris-venice-9723222, accessed December 2019.
21 KPMG, Room for improvement. The KPMG survey of business reporting, 2nd edition, 28 April 2016, available at: https://home.kpmg.com/xx/en/home/insights/2016/04/kpmg-survey-business-reporting-second-edition.html, accessed December 2019.
22 D. Brydon, Assess, assure and inform. Improving audit quality and effectiveness. Report of the independent review into the quality and effectiveness of audit, December 2019, pages 80–82, available at: https://assets.publishing.service.gov.uk/government/uploads/system/uploads/attachment_data/file/852960/brydon-review-final-report.pdf, accessed December 2019.

5 Disruption in reporting – the evidence

Evidence

This evidence represents a pre-pandemic period when there were a number of failures. Wirecard's problems were pre-pandemic, so it falls within this body of evidence. The advances in auditing will not, by themselves, prevent future scandals. Setting that aside, we now discuss other problems and issues with financial reporting and corporate reporting. So we have the Select Committee's statement:[1] 'Carillion's accounts were systematically manipulated to make optimistic assessments of revenue'.

And the committee commented that the stewardship and governance codes were insufficiently detailed to be effective and, they exist, completely unenforceable. A more active and interventionist approach would be needed in the forthcoming revision of these codes, including a more visible role for the regulators, principally the FRC/ARGA.[2]

And we like one of our reviewers' comments:

> If scandals are to be minimised – I doubt if they can ever be eliminated – greater use should be made of the existing powers. Culture will only change if all of those in the publication of financial statements – preparers and auditors alike – are faced with a proper and fair disciplinary regime.

Whatever the narrative and business model says, management probably still adhere to the principal of looking after the shareholders first and foremost. We found in our own collected evidence that this motive and objective was always present despite whatever the annual report might say. But that is not the real story. The underlying and principal motive is to retain their jobs and plans by not letting a hedge fund, private equity, or takeover specialist or rival make a hostile bid and take them over; and then fire many of the most senior management and, of course, the board. Elliot associates forced Whitbread to sell Costa Coffee (and split from Premier Inns) earlier than the company would have liked.

FRC Survey[3]

The FRC survey launched in October 2019, attracted 728 responses and more than 30,000 data points though just under a half were not completed (suggesting that the questionnaire may have been too long).

The report suggests that the potential users of corporate reporting and their objectives are more diverse than the conventional view suggests. Financial information is still the pillar of reporting. Websites are the preferred access point. Surprisingly the responses found that investor and non-investor views appear to converge on the majority of issues – something we did not find and do not necessarily concur with. (For example, not everyone wants to read the 20-odd pages of the remuneration report – though a proxy adviser thinking of organising a shareholders revolt would want to examine every word.) The FRC also found that many also rely on journalists and data aggregators as information intermediaries.

Users used reports more like an encyclopaedia than a novel when looking for content that matters to them. Focussed reports are likely to attract higher levels of engagement from users – such as existing highlights sections, financial statements, and strategic reports rank among the most thoroughly read items.

Reports were too long and about 20% of the users specifically unprompted would like to disaggregate information for more targeted use and access. However, the survey found that there is also a clear demand for revisiting and developing reporting on liquidity, intangibles, risks, audit related matters, stakeholder relationships, climate, workforce risks, and social and environmental impacts.

The FRC confirmed our observation that financial information has less to do with valuation than certain non-financial information (for example the number of active users/subscribers).

Length

Rod Sellers and Krish Bhaskar go on to say that they flinch at the sight of annual accounts running to hundreds of pages – 'seeing the wood for the trees' comes to mind. Rod Sellers goes on to express:

> 'After almost 50 years involved in preparing or studying accounts – during my working life as an accountant in industry and subsequently as a portfolio non-executive director – I am intrigued by the marked changes

and expansion in Annual Reports and Accounts over the last 10 years or so'. This is partly due to the reaction of the Global Financial Crisis and will be increasingly so with greater regulation and the incessant churning out of Big Data and also political and cultural developments.

We are not arguing for less information and disclosures, just that it be structured in a different way and easier to digest for a variety of different audiences. As we said, not all users of reports will want to read all the details of the numerous pages of the director's remuneration report.

Views and critiques

What the Big Four say

You would expect the Big Four not to be too critical of their major clients. And indeed that is the case, as personified by Appendix 3.05.1 What the Big Four say. The major contributors to these critiques are Deloitte and EY, though we use the awards given by PwC to offer our own critique of the best reporting companies (as judged by PwC's review).

Deloitte[4] uses such words as 'poor', 'misplaced', 'hides underlying truth', 'inadequate', even 'hopelessly inadequate'. By and large, we found that the main users of the narrative section are analysts and journalists, though analysts say they rely on personal contact and briefing by company management.[5]

EY made the interesting point that investors and others obtain information about companies from a variety of sources. However, annual reports remain the primary source of holistic information about a company, particularly for investors making an initial investment decision. There is scope for improvement in the consistency and balance of messaging across preliminary results announcements, analyst presentations, and the annual report.

What the reporting companies say

Appendix 3.05.2 What the reporting companies say and their conclusion is that it is system in crisis. This is a report from 977 senior financial officers from many industries in Europe and North America – the Future of Financial Reporting: Insights from the FSN Modern Finance Forum on LinkedIn – FSN/Workiva Survey 2017. Full details are provided in this appendix (3.05.2). Their opening summary is:

- More than 50% of respondents said reporting involved huge amounts of manual checking every time a change is made.

- 43% of the senior finance executives surveyed don't even know how many business-critical spreadsheets are in use.
- 60% of respondents said they spend too much time cleaning and manipulating data.
- 40% of boardrooms do not have a complete view of the business.

CFOs have lost their overall grip on reporting – too many changes too quickly to be thoroughly absorbed. There is too much manual checking and far too great a reliance on spreadsheets, which are prone to errors. Only 61% of senior finance executives say the board always has a complete view of business performance; 39% do not.

This survey takes the viewpoint of the preparers of the financial and corporate reports. From their viewpoint, it is a question of not being able to keep up with technology, the pace of regulatory change, and being faced with inadequate internal controls at a time when accounting and finance are being squeezed to reduce their headcount.

Spreadsheet woes

The survey found too much reliance on spreadsheets, with inappropriate use of spreadsheets to counteract failing IT systems, and 71% of organisations depend on spreadsheets for collecting data across the majority of their business units.

The FT[6] reinforced this earlier survey with an opinion and data. The article gave examples such as:

- A forgotten negative sign once led Fidelity's Magellan fund team to miscalculate a loss of $1.3 billion as a gain.
- JPMorgan Chase's $6.2 billion trading losses in 2012 – the 'London Whale' incident – were traced back to mistakes in the financial model used to calculate the risks associated with the trades.[7]
- Marks and Spencer in 2016 announced that sales had risen in the quarter. They had actually fallen – a spreadsheet error.
- A study of 15,770 spreadsheets used by Enron found nearly a quarter of those containing formulas were flawed.
- Conviviality could blame the trigger to its eventual demise on spreadsheet errors[8] – an error of up to £10 million.

The FT article goes on to analyse the probability of mistakes in spreadsheets. With more cells, the probability of errors increases exponentially:

The chances of making a mistake in any particular cell are small – likely to be in the range of 1 per cent to 5 per cent. But errors cascade down to subsequent cells, so the bottom line in large spreadsheets is highly likely to be wrong.

The best fix is thorough testing, as most textbooks will tell you. Making sure that all the rows or columns are added up correctly and that formula or conditional statements and indirect addresses are all meant to do what they were designed to do. There is a counter-argument put forward by this FT article:

> That [testing] is all time-consuming. Some managers do not understand or care. The boss of cartoon toiler Dilbert thought spreadsheet mistakes were fine, provided the final number was the one he wanted. How many times does that approach go undetected? Lots, probably.

Additional reporting requirements and pressure on management

There is one more issue. Given the pressure that reporting is currently placing on management, and then adding two new requirements of gender pay gap and supplier payment practices, this places an additional burden and a new method of reporting. Both these requirements may be quite onerous in new data collection and modification of data collection and information systems. Then there may be additional analysis that has to be performed to meet these requirements of both laid down by the government and some using definitions that are not usual in the commercial world. Remember, not to report or to report incorrectly is a criminal offence. Krish Bhaskar believes that there might be a certain fudging of the numbers for some organisations.

The now-famous Deloitte's annual report is more factual on the presentational trends of annual reports. The FSN/LinkedIn report is a cross-section of preparers' and managements' views. It might not be representative in being a stratified sample. It was respondent driven. But their report too demonstrates the disrupted and even broken nature of the financial and corporate reporting process. It is another tale of woe.

Bypassing the watchdogs and auditors

The gender pay gap and the payments practice are the first metrics to bypass the FRC (and the auditors) and hand control respectively to (a) the Equalities Commission and (b) the department of business. But there is more to come. The Insolvency Service will be asked to take a larger role in pursuing directors under the new governance code. The directors have a duty to a wider set of stakeholders and can no longer ignore actions and events after they dispose of a business.

In the future, that may catch the BHS sale for £1; Sir Philip Green (or his wife) were held accountable for subsequent losses and pensions liabilities. By the end of 2020, there were many failures, Debenhams and Sir Philip Green's Arcadia included. With Arcadia, we might see a repeat of the BHS issue. With a shortfall in the defined benefit pensions scheme estimated at around £350 million, Lady Green (Monegasque resident) is reported to be willing to make up some of the shortfall (around £100 million in several tranches). Will that be sufficient?

ICSA Report

ICSA (the Institute of Chartered Secretaries and Administrators) is the professional body for governance. Their report found that companies were divided on the quality of annual reports.[9] Of the 39% that said that companies are required to disclose too much information in their annual results, they mentioned (a) self-congratulatory waffling and (b) regulators being too isolated from real business life. Only 22% said that the annual reports were not useful for stakeholders, and their reasons included (a) they disclose too much information and (b) the annual report has become a source of 'obsolete information and unnecessary expense'. That said, 78% said the information was 'extremely useful' and gave investors and others a comprehensive understanding of the company, its culture, its business, and its longer-term prospects.

Importance of quarterly and half-yearly reports

Real-time reporting

Several partners at the Big Four were in favour of reporting on a continual basis in more or less real time, for example, daily or weekly of like-for-like retail sales. That might work in the retail arena. But in general, we found there were a variety of views. PwC's views on real-time reporting were documented in a PwC paper,[10] though that paper is no longer available online. In general, in our interviews, we found that with real-time data, there was only some limited support in certain sectors and certain types of companies. Real-time sales data may be relevant and a useful indicator, but it does not replace or supplant annual reports. It would be an addition.

More frequent reporting than annual

One study's findings[11] suggest that frequent reporting can impose significant costs by inducing myopic behaviour and distorting managerial investment decisions. The empirical results in the paper suggest that firms significantly reduce investments following an increase in reporting frequency. Specifically the report found, firms that increase their reporting frequency reduced their investments in fixed assets by 1.7% of total assets. This is an economically significant decline, as it builds up over several years. The reduction in investments is persistent up to at least 5 years and is robust for a range of alternative proxies for investment opportunities. And the report also concludes:

> We contribute to the literature on managerial myopia. Prior studies identify different sources of capital market pressures that can induce myopia. We suggest that frequent financial reporting is another mechanism that can encourage myopic managerial behavior. Our findings offer a starting point to evaluate this cost-benefit tradeoff by highlighting a significant cost of frequent reporting apart from the myriad benefits reported in prior research.

Another study in the Accounting Review examined the question of whether frequent financial reporting led to better or worse managerial decisions. Estimates indicate that increased reporting frequency is associated with an economically large decline in investments. Additional analyses reveal that the decline in investments is most consistent with frequent financial reporting inducing myopic management behaviour.[12]

Our conclusions from our evidence

This summarises what we found in our interviews and written evidence. This is not a proper sample or statistical study but more a large collection of anecdotal evidence:

> Annual – everyone agreed that there should be a core annual report.
> Quarterly reports – interestingly, we found that of the people and users we discussed this report with, they universally did not like this report. Type of myopia or short-termism was a common complaint reinforcing the academic research in the previous sections. On the other hand, it did remind management of the need to make profit and other warnings to the market in a timely fashion. But as the studies above show, it develops a short-termism which limits shareholder value in the medium and longer terms.
> Half-yearly reporting – Difficult to summarise. Interviewees were slightly pro to neutral and a few strongly against. Rod Sellers is especially keen on this report. John Flower is against. If there has to be a choice between half-yearly or more forecasts, Krish Bhaskar would prefer more on forecasts.

Real-time data – Some agreed with PwC's assessment that in certain sectors and certain types of companies, real-time sales data may be relevant and a useful indicator.

Mary Barth, in an article titled 'The Future of Financial Reporting: Insights from Research',[13] asked the question:

> . . . what does the future of financial reporting look like if we incorporate insights from research? I envision more fair value; a performance statement designed to highlight the information embedded in changes in fair value; information to help investors assess the value of intangible assets; more specific information about risk and uncertainty; information that is unbiased, rather than conservative; acceptance of a degree of earnings management together with a determination of how much earnings management is acceptable; and a financial reporting package that is purposefully designed to convey information users need, which presumably is broader than today's financial statements.

See Appendix 3.05.3 for a note on increasing borrowings and leverage/gearing.

Narrative: prevailing culture and impression management

The concept of impression management is: impression management uses the flexibility within the wider financial reports through the use of narrative, tables, diagrams, drawings, and graphs to convey a particular view to serve the interests of report preparers and management.[14]

What needs to change?

In nearly all of the recent cases mentioned in that volume, the annual report contained much glossy material, 'self-congratulatory waffle' (as per the ICSA report), boilerplate statements, and simulacra proclaiming the benefits of the company and how well they were doing. This is at worst nothing more than a biased, self-aggrandisement of the management, their role, and their performance.

Annual reports seem to contain so much 'noise' that the underlying performance is swamped by words extolling the virtues of the company, and, in particular, the management. This has become not just the norm but also the standard mantra of the FTSE 100 and many of the next 250 largest companies, the FTSE 250. This has become a cultural issue. The notion of balanced is, of course, subjective, but the over-riding sense, we feel, is that this is weighted significantly towards the interest of (a) the directors and a poor second (b) the shareholders.

Of the annual reports surveyed (our non-scientific sample of more than 100 but quite inclusive nevertheless[15]), the majority of the front-end narratives included a President Trump style of self-aggrandisement, self-congratulatory and boiler-plate type text with the flavour and tone subtlety positive regardless of what the figures show. Often (around 30%), we found, that the narrative is definitely not consistent with the financial figures – despite being signed off by the auditors that it is.

Scientific evidence is shown in Box 5.1. Boiral's conclusions were that a total of 90% of the significant negative events were not reported, contrary to the principles of balance, completeness, and transparency of GRI (Global Reporting Initiative) reports. Moreover, the pictures included in these reports, showcasing various simulacra clearly disconnected with the impact of real underlying business activities (for example, major strikes or industrial relation issues being swept under the carpet).

Box 5.1 Boiral paper summary

Olivier Boiral (2013), "Sustainability reports as simulacra? A counter-account of A and A+ GRI reports", *Accounting, Auditing & Accountability Journal*, Vol. 26, Issue 7, pp. 1036–1071.

Purpose – The purpose of this paper is to examine the extent to which sustainability reporting can be viewed as a simulacrum used to camouflage real sustainable-development problems and project an idealised view of the firms' situations.

Design/methodology/approach – The method was based on the content analysis and counter-accounting of 23 sustainability reports from firms in the energy and mining sectors which had received application levels of A or A + from the Global Reporting Initiative (GRI). The information disclosed in some 2,700 pages of reports was structured around 92 GRI indicators and compared with 116 significant news events that clearly addressed the responsibility of these firms in sustainable-development problems. Moreover, the 1,258 pictures included in sustainability reports were categorised into recurring themes from an inductive perspective.

Findings – A total of 90% of the significant negative events were not reported, contrary to the principles of balance, completeness, and transparency of GRI reports. Moreover, the pictures included in these reports showcase various simulacra clearly disconnected with the impact of business activities.

Originality/value – The paper shows the relevance of the counter-accounting approach in assessing the quality of sustainability reports and questions the reliability of the GRI's A or A + application levels. It contributes to debates concerning the transparency of sustainability reports in light of Debord's and Baudrillard's critical perspective. The paper reveals the under-explored role of images in the emergence of several types of simulacra.

www.emeraldinsight.com/doi/abs/10.1108/AAAJ-04-2012-00998

Boiral's findings have been replicated by more than 20 studies. The most recent work is by Melloni and is discussed in what follows.

However, there are further academic and scientific studies using multivariate and textual analysis, which confirms that the tone of a report and the amount of fogginess are statistically significant predictors of reported financial performance. Foggier means significantly longer and less readable and with less information, less complete. Often what we refer to as 'unbalanced' is better described by tone – defined as deliberate manipulation of the thematic content. Verbal tone manipulation was used in our sample as an impression management strategy.

Let's examine some samples. This is not a statistical study but more anecdotal. However, it is readily discernible in any random sample of the top FTSE 350 you care to choose. We feel that the best way to deal with this issue is to concentrate on specific identified cases in which the narrative reports give a view very different from the financial statements. These could be analysed between (a) cases in which the different view is justifiable and (b) cases in which it would seem to be unjustified.

PwC examines annual reports and each year produces an Excellence in Reporting Awards. In the 2015 award winners, there were three companies that Flower and Bhaskar examined in detail: United Utilities (joint winner in the FTSE 100 category), Tullow Oil (highly commended in the FTSE 250 category), and HMRC (highly commended in the public sector). However, we comment on one other (Carillion) in passing. See Appendix 3.06.4 for a detailed discussion of several specific examples of misleading narrative reporting.

Clues form the narrative as to real underlying performance

A scientific study about the tone of the narrative was made by Clatworthy and Jones in 2006.[16] The study assessed the effect of financial performance on the textual characteristics of the chairman's statement. In particular, given the increased motives for poorly performing management to engage in impression management, the paper focuses on whether companies' reporting strategies depend on underlying financial performance.

The first major feature is differential patterns of textual characteristics and company performance in the chairman's and other senior management narrative reports. The financial performance and results affect what is written.

The conclusions included:[17]

> 'This study investigates the narrative reporting practices of 50 highly profitable and 50 highly unprofitable listed UK companies. We find differential patterns of reporting in the chairman's statement contingent upon whether the companies are profitable or unprofitable. Compared with profitable companies, unprofitable companies focus less on key financial indicators, use fewer quantitative results, fewer personal references and more passive sentences, and focus more on the future'.
>
> ' . . . the results suggest that subtle textual characteristics are leading to good and bad news being treated asymmetrically'.

Their conclusions were reinforced by a more recent paper referencing many more articles on the narrative texts and bias in 2017[18] and by Leung, Parker, and Curtis in 2015.[19]

Although using Hong Kong data, the latter study found that minimal narrative disclosure in annual reports was a deliberate impression-management strategy to conceal information and explanations about persistently poor firm performance and future prospects to distract investors' attention from a firm's weakness or negative news – a bit like M&S failing to mention a turnaround plan in 2015 to 2017 (not that it did, but the group did fail to mention how bad the underlying situation actually was).

UEA and the Melloni scientific study[20]

This research tested hypotheses scientifically on a large sample of 148 integrated reports from 74 unique firms. The study found that firms with weak financial performance tend to be significantly longer and less readable (i.e. less concise) and more optimistic (i.e. less balanced). Their evidence implies that firms can employ quantity and syntactical reading ease manipulation as well as thematic content and verbal tone manipulation as impression management strategies. That just reinforces what we have said earlier.

In their literature review, they quote an extensive number of academic and scientific studies which show active impression management through the manipulation of narrative and figures.[21]

Narrative evidence – not fair or balanced?

Our empirical analyses also seems to indicate that levels of conciseness, completeness, and/or balance in annual reports seem to be associated with a problematic or weaker company's performance. This relationship confirms an active impression-management and disclosure strategy. This obfuscation strategy seems to be widespread and can be detected in many narrative disclosures examined in annual reports. If anything, as the economic environment becomes more difficult, this 'impression-management and disclosure' obfuscation seems to be increasing.

It is not a question of telling an authentic story, as one interviewee put it. For us, it is a matter of giving a fair, balanced, and honest tone and flavour to the assessment of what shareholders, professional investors, and other stakeholders want to know. Balanced and neutrally fair, rather than what the directors want you to believe. And not by omission. The narrative section is subjective. It is a matter of tone. However, the evidence does point to the view that the tone is not balanced, not neutral, and not even fair.

This is where we take issues with the FRC – these reports are not balanced. The audit of financial statements, we maintain after much empirical study, is not consistent with the words and the front end of an annual report – though they may not go as far as being a material misstatement. Usually, the auditors chose to say nothing is amiss (or note an exception). That said, frequently this is subjective, and any fair-minded person would raise an objection – like Tullow Oil, United Utilities, Carillion, M&S, John Lewis, and more than 100 others (in the 2017 to 2019 annual reports). Interestingly, the private companies (Arcadia, JCB, and so on) are often more balanced and honest (our casual anecdotal empirical conclusions).

The soft requirement

In theory, the narrative report on long-term viability (greater than 1 year) should have the following requirements for external auditors, according to

Deloitte.[22] This is common to many of the narrative sections, and these are soft requirements:

1 First, auditors must review the statement for consistency with the other knowledge they have acquired during the audit, including the assessment of going concern and whether the disclosures are in harmony with the overall requirement for the annual report to be fair, balanced, and understandable.
2 Second, auditors have a significant new requirement to report in the audit report whether there is anything material to add or draw attention to in respect of the directors' confirmation that they have carried out a robust assessment of principal risks; the disclosures that describe those risks and how they are being managed or mitigated; the going-concern statement and the longer-term viability statement.

This sounds good, but the practice is in reality for auditors to rubber stamp just about anything, we have found, even where the words definitely do not match the financial statements part of the annual report. Take any retailer in the time period 2016 to 2020 reporting year – and that is almost certainly true in our view. On the short-term, narrowed view of going-concern (up to 1 year) assessment, the FRC[23] had to release a further clarification after years of audit scandals (and even more FRC guidance at the end of 2020). Of course, we do not know what goes on behind closed doors. So the auditors may have exerted influence to take out or soften the most extreme statements which cannot be supported by the financial statements. However, using commonsense English, we found these two principles above for viability audit sign-off were not being upheld in many cases. This may now be tightened by the FRC/ARGA.

Impression management has become the culture and the mantra for managements to use various platitudes and expressions to manage and manipulate the material in the annual report and often to blow their own trumpet. In some cases the audit firms actually write or rewrite the annual report narrative. We found that auditors allow management to say just about anything in words without any comment – even if it is inconsistent or at odds with the financial statements. As with Carillion, auditors use the device of judgement on material misstatement. However, not everyone agrees. One auditor when reviewing this book made this comment:

> I do not agree with this comment. First material misstatement is not a device but a judgment in the eye of the beholder. It is a judgment that is properly made. We are back again into the expectation gap – what is actually expected of auditors and accounts compared to what they are required to do.
>
> Second the obligations are really quite limited. . . . My impression is that they are referring to the specific reports the directors have to make

and not about the other general marketing narrative on which you base most of your comments.

Those comments were referenced to various parts of the narrative statements. However, we have also provided the general test given and one provided by another reviewer. In brief, the external auditor has a duty to read the other information and consider if it is consistent with the results of the audit and, if not, whether it is materially misleading. The Big Four, in general, will probably disagree with our view. However commonsense interpretation of English would agree with our conclusions.

The hard requirement and the signing of the report

Of course, the financial statements and the rest of the annual report are only signed sometime between a few weeks to several months later than when they are prepared – usually 2 to 4 months after the year end.

When the auditors sign, they have to be satisfied of the hard requirement for the going concern. That is, management have to provide cash flow forecasts and other documents to satisfy the auditors of the going-concern hard requirement – that the company can survive for the next 12 months (recently strengthened by the FRC[24]). And there is a named signature from the senior or engagement partner of the audit firm, who signs the external auditor's report.

This was made clear by KPMG's letter to the select committee in respect of Carillion. That was the hard requirement. In our view, that letter only partially responded to the softer requirement as specified by Deloitte earlier. As in anything, this is just an opinion. Remember that there is a FRC investigation into KPMG's conduct in relation to Carillion and also at least one major court case against KPMG outstanding.

Narrative and corporate reports – way forward?

Our (and others) findings that there is virtually no constraint on what is said in the narrative section by management is an issue. This is despite the best efforts of the FRC to push for a fair and balanced test – namely the auditor's test of whether it is 'consistent' with the financial statements.

Given this meaning, the IAASB[25] has established a definition of an inconsistency in the other information. This specifies that such an inconsistency would exist when the other information:

a   Contains information that is incorrect, unreasonable, or inappropriate; or
b   Is presented in a way that omits or obscures information that is necessary to properly understand the matter being addressed in the other information.

Inappropriate can mean anything, so we can discount that word. Incorrect? Sales are increasing when they are not – that seems to be incorrect but is rarely commented on. Unreasonable is arguable and therefore can be dismissed. Omissions or obscuring reality – that, we found, is happening much of the time. However, what is the test for omission? Should it be the definition of 'material'? But this may have been set too high. From the evidence we have seen and is in the academic press, omission seems often to be the norm.

The FRC in its future of corporate reporting paper wants to make material variable according to the objectives of individual reports and as a whole of the total network of reports with justifications. An improvement over the older one size fits all philosophy.

But this is missing the point. A responsibility for the narrative is the preparer, the management, and the board and whomever they employ to create the narrative section (sometimes drafted by one of the Big Four or other smaller firms of accountants). Some of the Big Four seem to be particularly active in this area. So it is ultimately the board who should take responsibility and, despite their integrity or lack of it, it is evident they regard the narrative report as fair game. Many of the narrative studies we examined are now old, and the board has been at this impression management for many years. But recent ones include:

> . . . the fact can be employed to 'facilitate the construction of a new and different image of the company' and therefore improve its legitimacy in the wider world[26]
> . . . that narrative disclosures can be employed to 'facilitate the construction of a new and different image of the company' and therefore improve its legitimacy in the wider world.[27]
> . . . we observe that managers prefer accounting narratives rather than financial or other quantifiable information, because the former can be designed and customized to manage public impressions.[28]
> Regarding the relations between performance and conciseness and completeness/balance, our findings are in line with the impression-management argument empirically confirmed by previous studies in financial and environmental/sustainability reporting. In particular, firms with lower financial performance tend to produce longer, more complex reports unbalanced towards optimism.[29]

The big problem is *disentanglement*. The debate is complicated by the lack of convergence in the specialist literature on how to define and empirically *disentangle* disclosure quantity and quality.

Culture wrong – not just a question of tone?

We have commented that annual reports seem to be in the interest of management not shareholders. However, we also think there is a cultural issue. Anything seems to go in the narrative section. Few care about how this ties in with the financial statements. Fair, balanced, and understandable does not seem to being met at least in tone and degree of fogginess. Auditors can get away with this because they can say they have not identified material misstatements. That more or less excludes nearly all subjective statements or value judgements.

It is, however, a complex area. John Flower, for one, takes management's side. He feels it is not unreasonable for the directors to use their report to present their own viewpoint, which may be very different from that presented in the accounts – for example, that the company has a very rosy future because of the lucrative projects in the pipeline.

What limits should be placed on what they write? Clearly they should not tell lies. Though this has become blurred with the term 'fake news'. We think news-jacking should be out as well. This point is already partially covered in the audit report, where (for example, in the case of KPMG's report on Carillion 2016) the auditor reports that, with respect to the strategic report and the directors' report, they have not identified material misstatements. However, whatever they did do or not do, public perception now says it is not enough. Bear in mind that the audit report is only ever an opinion not a statement of fact.

There is also the problem in narrative reports about the aspect of omissions – whether deliberate or otherwise. This is always a value judgement.

We comment that we have found the narrative section to be too subjective, too capable of being manipulated, and too difficult for auditors to provide a valid and informative opinion. However, all the auditors we have spoken to claim they do care how the narrative information ties in with the financial statements. It is just that this is difficult to see when analysing many of the annual reports.

See Appendix 3.05.5 for the auditors' counter-view.

The FRC/ARGA view so far to 2019/2020

For the first time, the FRC may want to expand auditors' responsibilities by requiring them to examine companies' financial reports from 'front to back'. The FRC seems to be agreeing with our sentiment. In essence, post-Carillion, they now accept that there must be failings in the entire report. Their view is that front-half data can be very useful to stakeholders, but it is not audited to the same extent, and it is not done to a consistent standard. So the entire report should be audited in future to the same standard.

The criticism of the narrative section is not really tackled in the FRC's view of the future of corporate reporting (2020).[30] The new multiple reports have no solution to the tone, balance, honesty and fairness that we have highlighted. We tackle solutions to this problem in later chapters. The ICAEW has said that it is entirely possible for an auditor to give an opinion over the whole of an annual report and indeed argued the same (but not that strongly) in 2013. They argued that many people would like business information to be more trusted. Assurance on the entire annual report is a vital part of the solution to this problem. We are not sure that this ICAEW proposal would solve the problem.

The new enhanced proactive FRC and transformation into ARGA

In its new enhanced role, the FRC resolved a record number of cases in 2019/2020.[31] In its Annual Enforcement Review (AER) report,[32] the FRC claimed serval new events. However, the FRC gave the following reason for the major audit failures:

1   Insufficient involvement of the audit partner and over-delegation to junior members of the team
2   Disorganised audit work
3   Failure to step back and take an overall look at the financial picture
4   Auditor too close to management
5   Failure to involve the audit quality-assurance partner

The usual reasons. In the year 2019/2020, there were 88 cases examined by the FRC audit enforcement area. Most of the case enquiries are generated from horizon-scanning activities. This is a technique which includes FRC searches of listed company, Regulatory News Service (RNS) updates, and FRC review of the financial press. Other sources of enquiries for the FRC include complaints, whistleblowing disclosures, and referrals from other FRC teams, regulators, and professional bodies. There are three possible outcomes to a case:

a   Conduct committee usually dealing with serious investigations and ending with fines or sanctions
b   Constructive engagement, in which cases are resolved without an investigation or an enforcement action (i.e. fines or other sanctions). So it is a quiet word with the audit firm and teams involved. Usually this is a minor technical breach or where there is no real harm to investors (but not necessarily to other stakeholders).
c   No further action.

FRC/ARGA and corporate reporting

The transformation to ARGA is a given even though the political will and timetable may not be so clear-cut.[33] It is often forgotten that the FRC's activity includes all aspects of financial reporting and the regulations of the reports made to the public or subsets of the public (e.g. analysts). The regulatory body has a new Regulatory Standards Division that brings together our work in setting and influencing standards and codes and promoting best practice, including international influencing and investor and other stakeholder engagement.[34] There is now almost a continual drip of changes to reporting standards/codes, governance regulations,[35] technical accounting issues, and IFRS and UK GAAP amendments. This drip may become a flow of new documentation. It will become increasingly difficult to keep up with all the new utterances of this regulatory body as it expands its roles. That said, these tougher new actions by the FRC/ARGA may do nothing to stop the expanding narratives sections of corporate reporting from being misleading.

Where are we?

In Chapter 4 we postulated that the way forward was hybrid accounting and reporting with one CORE report and many MORE reports. This dovetails in with the FRC three core reports (Business, Financial Statements and the Public Interest report) and their four types of MORE reports (Supporting detail, Standing data, Special Purpose and other periodic reports).[36]

In this Chapter 5, we have also summarised the evidence showing that mostly the narrative sections of the annual report have been biased, with issues as to tone and culture. These narrative sections should be audited and should not be glanced over and found to be merely 'not inconsistent' with the financial numbers. At the moment we feel the narrative section is seriously distorting the annual report. We disagree with the FRC survey in that some of the CORE reports fits all users and stakeholders. Their objectives may be entirely different and a single financial statements document may not meet all of the diverse needs of the entire envelope of all stakeholders.

Notes

1 Strategy and Work and Pensions Select Committees. Carillion. Second Joint report from the Business, Energy and Industrial Strategy and Work and Pensions Committees of Session 2017–19. HC 769. Published on 16 May 2018. by authority of the House of Commons., page 4, available at: https://publications.parliament.uk/pa/cm201719/cmselect/cmworpen/769/769.pdf, accessed June 2018.
2 Ibid. Paragraph 179.

3 FRC, The results of the FRC's initial survey from the online survey of FRC Stakeholders on the future of Corporate Reporting, *FRC News*, 8 October 2020, available at: https://www.frc.org.uk/getattachment/97c4336c-3cf2-4884-8bcf-1f9542572669/Survey-report-final.pdf, accessed October 2020.
4 Deloitte. Thinking Allowed – The Future of Corporate Reporting: Meeting the information needs of corporate stakeholders, July 2016, https://www2.deloitte.com/content/dam/Deloitte/ch/Documents/audit/ch-en-audit-thinking-allowed-future-corporate-reporting.pdf, accessed December 2020.
5 That seems to run counter to insider trading but is commonplace and not usually classified by the watchdogs as insider trading.
6 Lex, Spreadsheets: Catalogue of errors, *Financial Times*, 8 March 2020, available at: www.ft.com/content/de9a1105-5f68-4bdf-baf9-19be5801f17f, accessed March 2020.
7 This required data to be manually copied and pasted from one Excel spreadsheet to another.
8 K. Bhaskar and J. Flower, *Financial Failures & Scandals: From Enron to Carillion*, Routledge, 2019.
9 ICSA, The UK company secretary market survey 2018, *The Core Partnership*, April 2018, available at: www.core-partnership.co.uk/market-survey-2018/, accessed December 2018.
10 Audit of the future, James Chalmers, PwC, around 2013.
11 Real Effects of Frequent Financial Reporting Posted by R. Christopher Small, Co-editor, HLS Forum on Corporate Governance and Financial Regulation, on Friday, 19 September 2014.
12 Arthur G. Kraft, Rahul Vashishtha, and Mohan Venkatachalam, Frequent financial reporting and managerial myopia, *The Accounting Review*, Vol. 93, No. 2 (March 2018), pp. 249–275, https://doi.org/10.2308/accr-51838.
13 Mary E. Barth, The future of financial reporting: Insights from research abacus, *Journal of Accounting, Finance, and Business Studies*, Vol. 54, No. 1 (February 2018), available at: https://onlinelibrary.wiley.com/doi/abs/10.1111/abac.12124, accessed July 2018.
14 See Chapter 3, K. Bhaskar and J. Flower, *Financial Failures & Scandals: From Enron to Carillion*, Routledge, 2019.
15 Not published and less scientific than demanded by a referred article. Nevertheless, the overall evidence was overwhelming and substantial.
16 M A. Clatworthy and M. J. Jones, Differential patterns of textual characteristics and company performance in the chairman's statement, *Accounting, Auditing & Accountability Journal*, 2006, Vol. 19, No. 4, pp. 493–511, available at: https://www.emeraldinsight.com/doi/abs/10.1108/09513570610679100, accessed December 2018.
17 Ibid.
18 Maria-Silvia Sandulescu, Impression management: An international perspective, *Audit Financial*, 2017, 15. 605. 10.20869/AUDITF/2017/148/605, available at: www.researchgate.net/publication/321187829.
19 Impression management through minimal narrative disclosure in annual reports. S. Leung, L. Parker, and J. Courtis, Impression management through minimal narrative disclosure in annual reports, *The British Accounting Review*, Vol. 47, No. 3 (2015), pp. 275–289.
20 Gaia Melloni, Ariela Caglio, and Paolo Perego (2017). Saying more with less? Disclosure conciseness, completeness and balance in Integrated Reports.

Journal of Accounting and Public Policy, Volume 36, Issue 3, May–June 2017, pp. 220–238, available at: https://www.sciencedirect.com/science/article/pii/ S0278425417300285 https://papers.ssrn.com/sol3/papers.cfm?abstract_ id=2861056, accessed May 2020.

21 Ibid.

22 Deloitte, Governance in brief: The longer term viability statement – a "how to" summary guide, *The Deloitte Academy*, October 2015, available at: https:// www2.deloitte.com/content/dam/Deloitte/uk/Documents/audit/deloitte-uk-oct-2015-gov-in-brief-ltvs-how-to.pdf, accessed May 2020.

23 FRC, FRC strengthens Going Concern audit standard, 30 September 2019, available at: www.frc.org.uk/news/september-2019/frc-strengthens-going-concern-audit-standard, accessed May 2020. and several additions in December 2020, https:// www.frc.org.uk/news/december-2020/frc-highlights-importance-of-a-challenge-culture-i https://www.frc.org.uk/news/december-2020/frc-announces-its-thematic-reviews,-audit-areas-of https://www.frc.org.uk/news/december-2020/ new-research-supports-introduction-of-standards-fo though the audit firms are responding with enhanced measures to form their evaluation of companies' going concern assessments: https://www.frc.org.uk/news/november-2020/audit-firms-enhance-going-concern-assessments.

24 Ibid.

25 Exposure Draft, 2012, International Standard on Auditing (ISA) 720 (Revised), The Auditor's Responsibilities Relating to Other Information in Documents Containing or Accompanying Audited Financial Statements and the Auditor's Report Thereon, International Auditing and Assurance Standards Board, November 2012, available at: www.ifac.org/system/files/publications/files/ ISA-720-The-Auditor%27s-Responsibilities-Relating-to-Other-Information-in-Documents.pdf, accessed June 2017.

26 N. Brennan, E. Guillamon-Saorin, and A. Pierce, Methodological insights: Impression management: Developing and illustrating a scheme of analysis for narrative disclosures – A methodological note, *Accounting, Auditing & Accountability Journal*, Vol. 22 (2009), pp. 789–832, Synopsis available at: www.emeraldinsight.com/doi/abs/10.1108/09513570910966379, accessed June 2017.

27 A. G. Hopwood, Accounting and the environment, *Accounting, Organizations and Society*, Vol. 34 (2009), pp. 433–439, available at: www.sciencedirect.com/ science/article/pii/S0361368209000294, accessed June 2017.

28 D. Neu, H. Warsame, and K. Pedwell, Managing public impressions: Environmental disclosures in annual reports, *Accounting, Organizations and Society*, Vol. 23 (1998), pp. 265–282, available at: https://s3.amazonaws.com/academia. edu.documents/44987894/relevant_public.pdf?AWSAccessKeyId=AKIAIW OWYYGZ2Y53UL3A&Expires=1550519893&Signature=q%2BxI5F%2F0 MLX5rDYDvhB32Jqq6l8%3D&response-content-disposition=inline%3B%-20filename%3DMANAGING_PUBLIC_IMPRESSIONS_ENVIRON-MENTA.pdf, accessed June 2017.

29 Op.Cit. Melloni et al., 2017.

30 FRC News, FRC resolves record number of cases through constructive engagement, 31 July 2020, available at: www.frc.org.uk/news/july-2020/frc-resolves-record-number-of-cases-through-constr and www.frc.org.uk/getattachment/ d299042a-f14f-40eb-8889-7b44818cf53b/Annual-Enforcement-Review.pdf, accessed July 2020.

31 Ibid.

32 FRC, The future of corporate reporting discussion paper, *FRC News*, 8 October 2020, available at: https://www.frc.org.uk/news/october-2020/frc-publishes-future-of-corporate-reporting-discus, accessed October 2020.

33 FRC, FRC annual report 2020, 17 July 2020, available at: www.frc.org.uk/getattachment/d3201f4b-2946-4e50-aa27-3a131ae17750/Annual-Report-2019-20.pdf, accessed July 2020.

34 Ibid.

35 The FRC found a mixed picture as some companies have embraced the opportunities the revised governance code offers, the FRC has found in its Review of Corporate Governance Reporting that this was not consistent across the board. FRC 26 November 2020, available at: https://www.frc.org.uk/news/november-2020/reporting-on-the-new-corporate-governance-code-is, accessed December 2020.

36 Op. Cit FRC October 2020, The future of corporate reporting discussion paper.

6 Disruption in reporting and the new technology

New accounting systems based on new technology

The pace of technological change and disruptive technologies have, if anything, been accelerated by the COVID-19 coronavirus. Financial reporting will be largely effected via technological enhancements of the internet, self-service reporting, real-time capture of events, big data, the cloud, whatever replaces the cloud (such as edge or fog computing), the web, and the newer 'dark' or grey web (defined in Appendix 3.06.1). Will technology make the present unwieldy and largely unread printed reports become a relic of the past? Probably.

Enter artificial intelligence (AI) into the equation. AI may make a host of decisions for humans – including taking over some accounting, auditing, and reporting functions – or at least provide tools to change their very nature. From an earlier volume, a summary of IT developments can be found in Appendix 3.06.2 New Technology.[1]

The broader impact and reach of the new technology

The relationship between the fundamental economic functions of accountancy and technology is explored in this section. In principle, some believe that advances in technology have no impact on the fundamental problems facing accountancy that concern the conflicts of interests between the management of firms, investors, and other stakeholders. One possibility is that advances in technology enable accountants to perform their functions better. Another is that they eclipse the need for accountants in favour of data experts.

Uber, Amazon, iTunes, and Airbnb are examples of destructive technologies.[2] Take Uber as a preeminent example: Uber has few assets and no taxis, yet it has become the world's number one taxi/transport company, with estimated revenues at more than $80 billion in 2020.[3] It is worth billions despite having never made a profit – if anything, the losses are increasing. Uber joins CVS, GE, and Qualcomm in the US as the only US companies valued at more than $50 billion which reported annual losses in the 2018–2020 time frame.

Uber develops, markets, and operates the Uber ride-hailing mobile app, which allows consumers with smartphones to submit a trip request, which is then routed to drivers. As such, it could become a general transport or logistics/package delivery service. It is new technology that has allowed this and many other disruptive technologies to dominate an important slice of the market just as mobile phones transformed the communications market. The same goes for Airbnb and the hotel industry.

Google's Home Assistant, Amazon's Alexa, Microsoft's Cortana, and Apple's Siri are assistants which will soon incorporate a degree of artificial intelligence (AI). Later, they will be hooked up to massive generalised AI systems, which will be able to do virtually anything (if permitted). Such adaptive systems will be, as they are today, your assistant and capable of helping you do whatever you want. We say permitted because it is likely that some form of regulation may be introduced.

Accelerating rate of new technology

We believe that through new technology and its impact, there will be an acceleration in how technology changes and affects all aspects of reporting in our medium- and long-term (2030 to 2050) time frames. What impacts reporting, we believe, will also feed back into accounting and thoroughly change auditing and the accountancy profession.

Technology can influence decisions by quickly bringing that information to a decision maker, who can offload shares – on an adverse profit warning, for example – ahead of the general market reaction and hence achieve a higher average sales price. Fractions of a second matter with automated trading. High-frequency trading in dark pools is virtually hidden from public view. As Michael Lewis writes in *Flash Boys*,[4] attempts to introduce a fairer exchange (called IEX) have not met with universal approval. So speed as measured in picoseconds (i.e. one trillionth of a second) still counts.

IT, the internet, new devices, and new technology pose major challenges for accounting, all aspects of reporting, and, of course, auditing. In general, all three areas have so far failed to take up the enormous opportunity of current technology, let alone future developments. This is one area in which the Big Four are powerless to compete for tech personnel with either the new tech giants (for example Alphabet [Google and Deep Mind (AI)] and Facebook), both with their new HQs in Kings Cross, London, or the smaller start-ups found in London's Silicon Valley (Old Street to Shoreditch).

The internet is not new, but it has matured. Now, with Web 2.0 and 3.0 well underway, the dark net and even the deep net cannot be ignored, nor are they solely concerned with criminal or pornographic information.

There are new data, events, records, and intelligence that never before existed. There are new ways to create data, clean data, add content to data, process data, store data, bring in social media, analyse data, do deep analysis on all the new data, and of course, present, report, and visualise this new data.

Financial, accounting, and bookkeeping systems

Double-entry bookkeeping has been with us for thousands of years. Luca Pacioli, a Franciscan friar, has been attributed with early usage, but there are signs that Muslim, Indian, and Egyptian use was far earlier than that.

When Krish Bhaskar headed up his department at the University of East Anglia, he tried to develop accounting in a way which gave rise to a subject area called 'computerised accountancy', but it never took off. The computer scientists, IT, and data processing professionals took over the development of software for accounting and have taken the lead in computerised accounting systems from then on – often expanding into management information systems and customer relationship management systems.[5]

Theories about what could replace double-entry bookkeeping have abounded, but none have worked or stuck. However, there are four enabling technologies or theories:

1   The concept of storing the event rather than filing it away in the form of an accounting ledger
2   Relational and entity-relationship accounting calling on computer science database theory
3   Triple-entry accounting
4   Blockchains – not to be confused with Bitcoins, other cryptocurrencies or anonymity, or even the dark web

Demise of double-entry accounting

It is true that the power and reliability of modern technology have greatly reduced the need for double entry's checking function ('the trial balance must balance'). But we believe that any system of reporting will include a statement of resources and claims at a specific point in time (that is a balance sheet) and a statement of performance over time (such as the income statement). The articulation between these two reports lies at the heart of double entry. We feel that it is useful to draw a distinction between double-entry bookkeeping (which is a way of organising and processing transactions) and double entry as a way of representing relationships between people. We are inclined to believe that double entry is a law of nature of the same order as the economist's law of diminishing returns – if Andrew borrows £10 in cash from Bob, Andrew's cash goes up and Bob's goes down. If Mary believes that her house has increased in value, both her wealth and the value of her house have increased.

Events accounting

A second earlier development, which has been adopted by many of the accounting software suites available, is associated with events accounting. The idea, simply stated, is that you don't keep a set of double-entry book-keeping entries; you record just the transaction or event and the sum of these to form whatever statement you want. There is no necessity to post and keep ledgers. This was first mooted by Sorter[6] and was soon followed by McCarthy – the principle author in this area. Normally events accounting is combined with database accounting.

Database accounting

Everest and Weber[7] applied relational database concepts to accounting. To derive relational models for both managerial and financial accounting, Everest and Weber took conventional accounting frameworks and normalised them (a standard relational procedure). They then illustrated the use of relational algebra operations to derive information from the normalised database.

They noted a number of issues:

1   The duality of double entry seemed at odds with efficient computer processing.
2   Also, the normalisation process embedded naming and classification artefacts in the database schema when it was applied to a conventional chart of accounts framework.
3   Much accounting theory concerns efficient classification schemes or naming conventions, whereas database management theory is more concerned with the objects to be classified.

McCarthy[8] developed a database accounting system to supposedly accomplish the better fit of accounting systems to advanced data structures. He did so by applying the entity–relationship (E–R) design process to the accounting domain. This resulted in a database schema with a higher level of semantic expressiveness and without embedded procedural aspects of conventional accounting.

The database orientation of data means that it usually has three conditions applied to it:

1   Data must be stored at the most primitive and granular levels.
2   Data must be stored such that entitled users have access to all of it.
3   Data must be stored such that it may be retrieved in various formats as needed for different purposes.

However, in order to meet the double-entry philosophy, one needs to add accounting and valuation rules to identify a statement of resources and claims at a specific point in time (that is a balance sheet).

McCarthy's subsequent accounting models

The McCarthy E–R (entity–relationship) accounting model draws upon Chen's E–R methodology[9] and starts with identification of entities that exist in the reality being modelled and proceeds with designation of relationships that connect those entities. If we discard 'artefacts' and concentrate on the real phenomena being accounted for, we find that accounting object systems are composed of three generalised groups of entities: (1) economic events such as sales and cash receipts, (2) economic resources such as inventory and cash, and (3) economic agents such as customers and vendors.

The semantic nature of identified relationships in the model can be ascertained by analysing both operating policy and practice. For example, the relationship between 'cash' and 'cash disbursement' is a one-to-many relationship indicating that all payments are made from a single account at a time. Alternatively, the many-to-many relationship between 'cash disbursement' and 'general and administrative service' could mean that the company's policy necessitates the most general case in order to facilitate prudent cash management.

Once an E–R model has been created, usually in the form of a diagram, Chen's modelling procedure moves to the more detailed level of design, examples of which are given in Appendices 3.06.3 – McCarthy's original examples. Such diagrams and tables indicate the characteristics of each entity/relationship set that are of interest to potential system users. They also illustrate which entity sets will play the roles required by each relationship. The declarative aspects of the E–R model form the base from which all accounting information is eventually derived. These aspects are the base objects of the model, and we presume that they consist of sets representing economic events, resources, and agents plus relationships between those elements.

The McCarthy REA (resource-event-agent) accounting model is a development of McCarthy's entity–relationship system and shows, in theory, how an accounting system can be adapted for the computer age.[10] This was originally proposed in 1982 as a generalised accounting model and contained the concepts of resources, events, and agents. This accounting framework was designed to be used in a shared data environment where both accountants and non-accountants are interested in maintaining information about the same set of phenomena. REA systems have usually been modelled as relational databases with entity–relationship diagrams and concepts. The REA model gets rid of many accounting objects that are not necessary in the computer age. Most visible of these are debits and credits – double-entry bookkeeping disappears in an REA system. Many general ledger accounts also disappear, at least as persistent objects, e.g. accounts receivable or accounts payable. The computer can generate these accounts in real time using the source document records (as in the source events), but for the philosophy of double entry you will need to add accounting, valuation rules, and formulae (or, in their absence, 'opinions').

IT specialists used what they needed from IT developments and modern database technologies. Accounting models, such as those of McCarthy and others, were more or less rejected. Double-entry bookkeeping was recreated for all modern accounting systems. If they were based on relational or other advanced databases, then the double-entry system was recreated as artefacts within the system.

Evaluation of McCarthy's E–R and REA accounting systems

We do not think there is much mileage in E–R or REA models of accounting systems. Both these models use techniques to embody the double-entry philosophy using a number of artefacts. They are logically neat, but they do not essentially move away from the double-entry philosophy whilst complicating the accounting models with a number of these creative artefacts to take the place of double-entry philosophy. There is one foundation element drawn from relational databases which we believe is vital for all future accounting systems and blockchain ledgers. Events accounting coupled with database techniques is, we believe, the only way forward. Whether you then recreate a double-entry system on top is not important.

John Flower feels it extraordinary that the foundations of the current techniques for employing modern technology in accounting were laid by accounting theorists some 50 years ago. Sorter and Co. were pure theorists – the ideas that they developed had nothing to do with technology, except they had to wait until the appropriate technology had developed before their ideas could be fully implemented.

Normalisation of data

Of all the concepts, it is perhaps normalisation of data that will live with us in accounting systems as we modify them for multiple entry – which we believe will be the main type of the more modern accounting system. Database normalisation is the process of structuring a relational database in accordance with a series of so-called normal forms in order to reduce data redundancy and improve data integrity. See Appendix 3.06.3 Normalisation of data for an example of this process.

Triple-entry accounting

Triple-entry accounting, sometimes called momentum accounting, was first conceived by Yuji Ijiri.[11] It presents a framework for a new way to do accounting, uses the standard double-entry system with the usual debit and credits, and then adds a third entry, which represents changes in balances; these three items are then recognised events. Wikipedia provides an example:[12]

> An acceleration in revenue earning, such as a $1,000 per period increase of revenues from $10,000 per month to $11,000 per month, is a recordable event that would require three entries to implement.

Essentially, Yuji has taken the familiar concept and added some new concepts to provide more information about where the organisation is headed. The idea is that accounting could be fundamentally tied to forecasting. This is a concept which did not prove popular and is not currently used.

Triple-entry concept by Ian Grigg – the digitally signed receipt

This triple-entry (actually in reality multi-entry) accounting concept was proposed by Ian Grigg in 2005.[13] This is an entirely different concept. It can be illustrated with the following example, as shown in Figure 6.1. Instead of physically signing a receipt, this uses a digital signature and a key for encryption. When Alice wishes to transfer a value to Bob in some unit or contract managed by Ivan (the intermediary server), she writes out the payment instruction and signs it digitally, much like a cheque is dealt with in the physical world. She sends this to the server, Ivan; he agrees and does the transfer in his internal set of books. He then issues a receipt and signs it with his signing key. As an important part of the protocol, Ivan then reliably delivers the signed receipt to both Alice and Bob, and they can update their internal books accordingly.

The digitally signed receipt, together with the authorisation for a process for a transaction, represents a modification of double-entry bookkeeping,

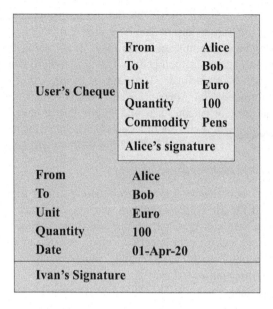

Figure 6.1 A Signed receipt

at least at the conceptual level. The cryptographic invention of the digital signature gives powerful evidentiary force to the receipt and, in practice, reduces the accounting problem to one of the receipt's presence or its absence. This problem is solved by sharing the records – each of the agents (Alice, Bob, and Ivan) has a good copy.

Grigg noted that in terms of relational database theory, double-entry bookkeeping is now redundant; it is normalised away by the fourth[14] normal form. Fourth normal form is a level of database normalisation in which there are no non-trivial multivalued dependencies other than a primary key. In this scheme, relational databases, encryptions, digital signatures, and double-entry bookkeeping work together and in harmony. That said, it is a small step from this concept to blockchain accounting. This has been claimed as a dramatic change to double entry. It is not. It is just a modification or an extension.

Blockchains

Do not worry about the definitions. It is just a glorified file with some special properties. Forget cryptocurrencies (such as Bitcoin and its major rival, Ethereum) – there are more than 1,000 cryptocurrencies and growing continuously – though these may change by 2030 (when we suspect some concentration will have occurred). Think of it as a glorified digital ledger. Okay, it is distributed, so it is resilient – it can't be taken out by a number of nodes failing and transactions or data is verified without any central authority (in our previous example there are many Ivans doing the processing which should all agree) – although it isn't quite as foolproof as some claim. By 2030, it will be mainstream. That said, as mentioned, it's no big deal. For more information, see Appendix 3.06.4 on blockchains. Of course, this raises the question of whether it would be possible to have industrywide, countrywide, or a worldwide set of ledgers/blockchains (as in Bitcoins).

Blockchains and multi-entry accounting

Multiple-entry booking, as opposed to double entry or triple entry, is a system geared for use with blockchains and large databases, albeit using relational database concepts and normalisation, for efficiency (eliminating redundancy) and for data integrity. This is akin to having a relational database with double-entry bookkeeping, signed receipts, every transaction stored in three places (Alice, Bob, and Ivan the server, or debit, credit, and the blockchain miners[15]). Then that data is normalised in some sort of relational form, or it could be simpler – additional information relating to different valuations, characteristics of the transactions, and any other data, including notes about future or market values. The analytics of web information could be added if brought online, including whether this is a returning or new customer and the length of time it took him or her to buy, the number of times visited before buying, and so on. However, this places a greater emphasis on the data that is entered into the blockchain.

Blockchain accounting and blockchain information systems are just examples of several new developments. Very great resources have been made available to the average user of financial information (whether shareholder or other stakeholder). These resources include great and local computing power, comprising the capability to perform complicated calculations and procedures and being able to access vast quantities of data through the internet. This enables (in theory) the user to be self-serving and the possibility of preparing his or her own accounts.

Distinction between preparer and user

That means that the distinction between preparer and user that lies at the foundation of much of the theory of financial reporting is being broken down. The use of the raw data plus the accounting/valuation rules means that the distinction between the two becomes more blurred.

Accounting and business computer technologies that will affect reporting

We have noted that so far, reporting has failed to keep up or make any headway amongst the new developments now reviewed. We now have the internet, social media, big data, cloud computing, edge computing, smartphones, and tablets as epitomised originally by Apple's iconic iPhone and iPad and now copied elsewhere, and such streaming services as Netflix, Amazon Prime, and Sky's Now TV. However, everything changes. Tablets are losing ground to the ever-larger smartphones. Even laptops have lost share to smartphones.

Of course, social media and smartphones, smart watches, smart glasses, and other smart wearables are only a step in the exponential rise of IT devices and applications that have inextricably become part of life. Generation Z and Generation Alpha social groupings will be born with such newer devices as toys – if they are not already doing so. What 10-year-old from a middle-income grouping does not now already have a smartphone in Europe and the US . . . and, for that matter, the middle classes in China, India, and most of Asia?

Then there is the reporting element. Increasingly this is web, cloud, and social media based, but none of this is as yet audited unless it has been enshrined within a single PDF (or equivalent) document which has been certified as being audited. Otherwise, anything on a website is considered fair game. There is no requirement to actually offer reliable and accurate information. Fake news is spread by social media – and sometimes by US presidents and other politicians! That said, as we add more reports and more information, including new and diverse non-financial information, the data volume will grow exponentially. So extracting information intra- or extra-company/organisation is going to require some new filtering and extraction techniques. The knock-on auditing implications are significant.

The new IT era will also break down a transaction or an event into finer and more granular components, discussed next. Meanwhile, think of a blockchain as a glorified ledger that may be shared by many users.

Impact on accounting and information systems

Let us recap the impact to accounting and information systems.

1   The emphasis shifts to the importance of data capture or data entry. If an error occurs at this point, then it is virtually locked into the system. The Internet of Things (IoT) captures the event in real time and uploads it to the cloud or equivalent.

2   The design of the basic structure of the system is a multi-entry record. Now it has to go to the lowest common denominator of possible information, including valuation method, alternative valuation methods, notes on the same, and any bit of data that might be used subsequently, given multiple objectives and multiple valuation methods and perhaps multiple accounting standards. Currency and relative range in value at the point of the transaction will also become vital. As with the time, the exact fraction of a second, the location, and the time stamp could be recorded.

3   That same basic record design may have to record new information, such as the definition of an employee such as defined in the gender-gap government measurement criteria or ethnicity and other criteria.

4   From the previous sections, we now know that the programming and coding are vital. Make a mistake and you open up your central records to hackers. Once created and signed off, that transaction code should be incapable of being modified, and any attempt to do so should sound an alert (though additional information and updates of, say, valuations, can be added). It should also be certified by some authority or even one of the larger accounting/auditing firms with some sort of guarantee. Change control will be vital.

5   Similarly, the master permissions, keys, and password, if compromised, mean that the whole information system may be compromised. Hackers tend to empty cash quickly. So once breached, you may have, at most, minutes to prevent money bleeding out. Perhaps just seconds . . .

6   Individual responsibility for the maintenance of keys and passwords is going to become critical. However, there is a danger. We have been locked out of Microsoft and Google Ads accounts despite having the right password, a security code sent to the correct email address, and a subsequent code sent to the correct mobile phone address in a text message . . . and the account can still remain blocked. Suspicious events such as different country or device settings may interfere and cause the system to block any access. It can be what can only be regarded as a nuisance.

In a way, although the processing is secure and can't be fiddled with (as long as there are several miners of identical computing power), the whole process, as shown by the various hacking examples of cryptocurrencies (so far the major blockchain application), problems, fraud, and errors still creep in. In fact, if a breach is made, the results are much more devastating. Millions can go within seconds. So the internal controls, internal auditing, and external auditing actually become more important, more exacting, and more critical. In this event, we suspect the external auditing role, not a statutory requirement but an auditing consultancy project, would become important and a potential fee-earning prospect for the Big Four and maybe beyond to the larger mid-tier accounting firms.

The problem of concentration

Suitably designed and programmed blockchain ledgers, unlike Bitcoin, which is inefficient and limited, can cover industries, countries, and even regions. If such a system is hacked and there are a large number of players, persuading someone outside the blockchain ledgers to do something that compromises the blockchain may be possible. As usual, the fraudulent, criminal element just moves on. See Appendix 3.06.5 for several frauds based and allowed by cryptocurrencies.

Self-service reporting

The most significant impact is to allow reports tailored to individual users, or classes, or for the users themselves, with suitable permissions, to generate their own report – the so called self-service reporting tool. Self-service reporting tools allow the user to access the original data and to pull whatever he or she wants in any desired format and aggregation.

This process has to train accountants and auditors to think of the people they serve as users – just like IT professionals. The data and the methods of extraction could be up to individual users or classes of users as being stakeholders. Different stakeholders will require different levels of permissions and different reports. There will always need to be a standard set of reports, consistent with the CORE and MORE introduced in Chapter 4 and the multi-report structure is now supported by the FRC.

Hybrid reporting encompasses both the CORE and MORE set of standard reports and also self-serving reports in which the users or classes of users can extract information according to their own criteria.

The importance of a single unique report

The CORE report is a single unique report. There are considerable advantages for society in requiring a person (an individual or a firm) to prepare a single unique report which sets out its position and performance (taxation, payments to different stakeholders, etc.). This ensures that the function of reports is to measure not only performance but also the distribution function.

Artificial intelligence

Machine learning occurs through repeated operations in which there is a series of outcomes which can be ranked (games such as chess, AlphaGo, and other such games). These games are in closed systems in which repetition can be performed and where there is a clear outcome even though the game may be played millions of times. One has to use techniques to dynamically refine the weights over time in the neural networks. Backpropagation is a technique to improve a neural network's accuracy. See Appendix 3.06.6 on artificial intelligence. However, repetition is not something that can always be found in the real world of business, accounting, and auditing. So AI will take longer, but we can envisage a reporting AI, an auditing AI, and an interrogation AI.

Use of grey information and leveraging these IT developments

Eccles and Krzus[16] claim that there is no reason companies and their audiences cannot use big data and analytics with cloud computing and social media to improve the creation, distribution, and consumption of 'integrated' reports. They also say that when the power and collaborative benefits of cloud computing are brought to bear on big data analytics' applications, using information generated from many different sources, companies can significantly improve their integrated reporting and thinking.

Big data does not replace traditional data and analytics. Conventional data sources, especially financial data, will still reign and be important. The new and grey data are additions which need to be handled with care. That said, this will lead to a change in priorities and challenges.

Future thoughts

This is what one enlightened member of the Big Four said:

> Above all of this is the future dimension you are seeking to consider. Technology is changing so fast and the accounting profession is not keeping up with it. I find it surprising that the desire for government transparency enables one to see, for example, a monthly spreadsheet of all payments made by The Home Office in excess of £25,000. If we have the millennial generation not bothered about privacy to the same extent as prior generations and we have the 'FinTech' start-ups using blockchain for authenticating transactions, where does this leave the traditional financial reporting model in 20 years' time? Do we end up with all transactions entered into by companies in some cloud type infrastructure, each transaction authenticated and given bespoke rights of access? Does that lead to producing financial statements with a series of SQL type statements? Or do financial statements become an irrelevance in such a model? Equally is audit an irrelevance if each transaction is authenticated at source? If you do have financial statements you will still need some period end 'valuations' of assets and liabilities. However, even that might bring about a different approach from regulators especially those in the banking sector

who have long had a desire for consistency between institutions e.g. a syndicated loan to company X, bank A and bank B are both members of the syndicate: A provides nothing against the loan and B provides 25%; this tends to result in an unhappy regulator of Bank A. Even then how relevant is all of the historical data for the future?

Impact of grey information on the accountant, investor, or auditor

There are a number of impacts and relevance of the new technologies to accountants, finance personnel, investors, and auditors.

1   Data and information systems will be spread across a wide set of central and distributed processing power and data storage.
2   Data collection will be via phones, fridges, all the IoT devices, wearables, and new handheld devices, and much of the data capture will occur in these distributed devices. So verification and control will be an order of magnitude more complex.
3   For decision making for professional investors, analysts, bankers, they are going to need to be able to trawl through the whole sea of grey data to check on progress, performance, management ability, and any operational problems as well as customer and supplier sentiments.
4   To check on stock and share price issues, the same group should be able to analyse succinctly the buy/sell decisions of shares. In addition, they need the ability to check on short- or long-sellers and similar such as hedging manoeuvres. (Shades of Carillion . . . such a system would have thrown up problems possibly as early as 2015.)
5   Internal and external auditors would need to trawl through all the grey information to check on problems, possible early signs of failure, support for the management's forecasts, hints of report manipulation, and anything inconsistent with the report of the entity they are auditing. The use of social media and the grey internet will become increasingly important.

Integrity and audit of input data

As mentioned earlier, it also implies a new task for the auditor – to vouch for the integrity of the data that is made available to the user and preparer. As ever, the acronym, GIGO (garbage in garbage out) is highly relevant. Note that fraud with cryptocurrencies has been rampant. Far from bringing security, they have enabled a new and large method of fraud – so far. The focus changes to data capture and then any set of accounting/valuation rules that is applied to the original events.

The audit of input data is an important issue. It changes the emphasis in auditing from checking the entity's system for processing transactions after they have entered the system to how they enter the system. Our comments on different sources of input data (point 2 above) are highly relevant but greatly complicate the issue. Any accounting/valuation rules would need to be checked if applied to that input data.

Expansion of the grey info

The expansion of the grey net and even the surface net is increasing exponentially. See Box 6.1 for the situation as of 2020. For third-world countries, the smartphone circumvents landlines and allows internet access. The world total is important because there are no borders with the internet. For example, pandorapick.com was a Chinese scam site trying to confuse itself with Pandora the jewelry maker, with a large online presence. *The Independent* mentioned a variety of problems with some Chinese websites.[17] Chinese and other Asian scam sites are still very much growing. Frequently they will display fabulous clothes which are then farmed out to rural workers who make cheap and shoddy copies of the display articles. Returns are seldom acknowledged.

Box 6.1   Selected current internet metrics

World population in 2020: officially 7.8 billion but taking into unmeasured Asian villages, the true figure is probably closer to 9 billion.[18] Figures below are authors' estimates:

Mobile phones: over 7 billion in 2020
Number of mobile devices: over 14 billion in 2020
Number of users in the web: over 6 billion in 2020
Number of pages that can be indexed in the surface web: over 1 trillion
Number of URLs: over 35 trillion
Number of domains/sites in surface web in 2020: 1.9 billion
Number of domains in deep and dark web in 2020: 1.3 trillion
Number of Facebook subscribers by end of 2020: 2.7+ billion
Number of TikTok subscribers by end of 2020: approaching 1 billion
Number of social media users in 2020: 4 billion
Number of cryptocurrencies in 2020: over 1,000
Number of ecommerce sites in 2020: between 12 and 24 million

FRC reporting and technology

The FRC,[19] and we would agree, proposes:

* A full set of corporate reporting schemas/structures to support tagging of all reports in the reporting network.
* A single storage location/data portal that works across regulatory reporting requirements (listed and unlisted companies) to provide a consistent and efficient source of regulated company data.
* New search and analytics tools that utilise the reporting network.

The FRC technology-enabled reporting would see all reporting content produced in a digital format as the default. There would be an option of printed copies and pdf. The various digital reports should be driven by the objective of the report and the FRC's system level attributes (i.e. accessibility, consistency, connectivity, and transparency). The digital format could include such mediums as HTML, video and PowerPoint. All reporting content would be tagged with relevant machine-readable tags. Tagging would be determined both by specific regulatory requirement and by a more general network of tagging requirements (that might evolve). The network tags would use XBRL and would communicate essential information about how the report/content fitted into the network, such as period, audit status, report type, report objective and so forth.

The FRC envisages that once tagged, the preparer would then file the report to a single public filing location (such as Companies House we think) and the company's website. The preparer would be able to connect and cross-reference across the submitted reports.

Where are we now?

There are going to be many changes which will reflect on financial and corporate reporting. Among other areas, we think the basic accounting system will be more related to storing events at the most granular form, capturing as much information as possible. So these basic records will be kept in multi-entry events-oriented databases with enhanced security (and this may or may not involve blockchains). The raw granular data may be interrogated directly to produce reports by applying differing accounting and valuation rules/methods by scanning all these basic records and applying differing aggregation and valuation rules. The cloud, social media, AI, and other developments outlined in this chapter will all contribute to new impacts on reporting. We outline those that might enable better reporting in the next three chapters.

Notes

1 K. Bhaskar, J. Flower, and R. Sellers, *Disruption in the Audit Market: The Future of the Big Four*, Routledge, 2019. Chapter 6.

2 A disruptive technology is one that displaces an established technology and shakes up an industry or a ground-breaking product that creates a completely new industry.

3 IPO valuation was $82.4 billion. At one point, it was being valued at $120 billion. In 2020, the market capitalisation is as low as $32 billion.

4 Michael Lewis, *Flash Boys: Cracking the Money Code*, London: W. W. Norton & Company and Allen Lane Penguin, 2014.

5 Of which the largest is Salesforce, then offerings by Oracle and SAP.

6 G. H. Sorter, An 'events' approach to basic accounting theory, *The* Accounting *Review* (January 1969), pp. 12–19.

7 Gordon C. Everest and Ron Weber, A relational approach to accounting models, *The Accounting Review* (April 1977).

8 E. W. McCarthy, An Entity-Relationship View of Accounting Models, *The Accounting Review*. October 1979, available at: https://msu.edu/~mccarth4/ar79.pdf, accessed December 2020.

9 P. P. Chen, The entity-relationship model – toward a unified view of data, *ACM Transactions on Database Systems*, Vol. 1 (March 1976), pp. 9–36.

10 E. W. McCarthy, E. W, The REA accounting model: A generalized framework for accounting systems in a shared data environment, *The Accounting Review* (July 1982).

11 Yuji Ijiri, Momentum accounting and triple-entry bookkeeping: Exploring the dynamic structure of accounting measurements, *Studies in Accounting Research*, Vol. 31 (1989), American Accounting Association, Sarasota.

12 Wikipedia, Momentum accounting and triple-entry bookkeeping, available at: https://en.wikipedia.org/wiki/Momentum_accounting_and_triple-entry_bookkeeping, accessed December 2020.

13 Grigg, I., Ripple Entry Accounting, *Systemics, Inc.,* 2005, available at: http://iang.org/papers/triple_entry.html, accessed August 2020.

14 Or higher normal forms.

15 A peer-to-peer computer process, blockchain mining (independent with Bitcoins) is used to secure and verify Bitcoin and other cryptocurrency transactions. With Bitcoins, there are several miners, and they should all have the same result. Their processing efforts are rewarded by a fee when actually used. Mining involves blockchain miners who add cryptotransaction data to the cryptocurrency's global public ledger of past transactions. If several participate, they should all have the same result.

16 R. G. Eccles and M. P. Krzus, *The Integrated Reporting Movement: Meaning, Momentum, Motives, and Materiality*, Wiley, 2014, page 269.

17 K. Forster, Disappointed customers expose cheap clothing 'scams' by sharing online shopping nightmares, *The Independent*, 13 November 2017, available at: www.independent.co.uk/news/business/news/disappointed-customers-expose-cheap-clothing-scams-by-sharing-online-shopping-nightmares-a6975201.html.
See also:
www.startbuyinginchina.com/fake-chinese-shopping-sites-black-list/
www.chinacheckup.com/blogs/articles/chinese-scam-reporting-websites
All accessed August 2020.

18 For example, there are large number of villages in the Indian subcontinent which are virtually inaccessible and cannot be counted. The same is true for other areas in Asia.

19 FRC, The future of corporate reporting: A matter of principle, FRC Discussion paper, *FRC News*, 8 October 2020, available at: https://www.frc.org.uk/getattachment/cf85af97-4bd2-4780-a1ec-dc03b6b91fbf/Future-of-Corporate-Reporting-FINAL.pdf, accessed October 2020.

7   Short-term remedies and quick fixes

Our short-term remedies and quick fixes

In terms of possible scenarios, there is only one conclusion: more and more regulations, eventually notwithstanding the wishes of the current government and Brexit deal. Failures will continue to occur, hastened in some cases by the pandemic and its aftermath, and regulations will, eventually, tighten. In that spirit, we offer our alternatives and recommendations. This is based on our combined knowledge and the evidence provided to us, our own original research and analysis. We also have taken the best ideas and solutions, in our view, found in the literature – including the latest FRC suggestions. In terms of recent reviews, we summarise the recommendations by the Kingman Review[1] and others in Appendix 3.07.1.

These are our 23 suggestions for some short-term remedies which might lead to better quality of financial and corporate reporting in the shorter run. Each 'quick fix' stands on its own so that one might cherry-pick the quick fixes that find favour, viewed appropriately, or might be adopted in some way from the bare bones outlined in what follows. Each is relatively easy to implement but may require more work from (a) management and (b) auditors. That, however, is the cost for better quality and safer reporting and auditing.

We assume the FRC transformation into ARGA is in place and that a part of the Kingman report[2] has been adopted and that there is an operational split between auditing and consultancy and that consultancy is banned from audit clients.

Greater control on management

Although Rod Sellers generally supports the integrity of management, the failures discussed earlier in the book (Volume 2: *Financial Failures & Scandals: From Enron to Carillion*)[3] as part of this series show that some boards and managements do have problems. The plethora of failures in 2019 and the more than 50 failures during 2020 described in www.fin-rep. org/which-book/financial-failures-scandals-from-enron-to-carillion/ show that financial scandals and failures, despite increasingly tightening regulation in the UK, are still occurring, and, if anything, are accelerating. That may be helped by COVID-19.

Tesco (overstated profits) may have been a case of not wanting to report lower profits in the face of new lower-priced competition. Conviviality was a case in which the systems lagged behind the growth of the company and the spreadsheets had not been sufficiently checked. (As the earlier surveys show, they were not the only ones.) Carillion's issue was an overestimate of revenues coming in and insufficient margins to cover problem contracts and too much debt – accumulated over time by aggressive accounting, perhaps. Steinhoff and Satyam were a pure management failure. General Electric was probably an internal reporting and management failure. Sig was employee related. Petrobras was corruption. In all these recent cases, there is a measure of management failure. Wirecard is a case in which senior management pulled the wool over the eyes of everyone – regulating bodies included. Only the whistleblowers, a hedge fund, and the FT saw through this deception. Then there are the overseas (often Chinese) companies.

Patisserie Valerie was a failure of multiple-faceted areas like lack of governance/controls, lack of information, and top management being unaware of what was going on in the whole arena of accounting, finance, and banking. There is even the hint of management being part of the whole debacle of a £40 million hole in the balance sheet and unauthorised bank loans of £10 million or so.

Coupled with these failures, we have found that the narrative section of annual reports is more often than not biased, unbalanced, not particularly fair (despite the FRC's pronouncements) and can have some notable omissions. This is a value judgement, of course, but our findings and evidence seem to show that this is not a one-off. For listed companies, this seems to be more the norm than the exception. That is not so true for private companies, for which the length is very short but fairer and more balanced (we found).

The short-term remedies on management and the preparers of reports

1) Penalties on management

FRC/ARGA needs to be able to prosecute directors whether they belong to a professional accounting body or not. Previously we noted the asymmetric nature of the approach to auditors and management (the situation faced by the old FRC). These should be made symmetric and not just to those members of a company that are part of one of the professional accounting associations. That would include members of boards and their major subsidiaries, the non-executive directors (NEDs), the internal auditing staff, and any external firm offering internal auditing as a service (*a la* Deloitte with Carillion). The NEDs and external service providers would be under scrutiny if they were not being sufficiently challenging or sceptical of the main board's or management's assumptions.[4] This seems to be the current direction of the government and new regulations.

As Fiona Wilkinson (ICAEW president in 2020) says, it is the fault of the directors:[5]

> We also need to remind the world that when companies fail unexpectedly, it's not primarily the fault of the auditors. It's a failure of corporate governance and, in the first instance, the fault of the directors. They should know when a company is no longer a going concern, but are they being transparent enough with the auditors? Possibly not. It seems to me that we need to step up the pace of culture change in the corporate world. This is why encouraging diversity (another issue close to my heart) is so important. We need people in the boardroom who not only bring insight from a range of social, educational and ethnic backgrounds but who are prepared to challenge 'group think'.

2) Temporary sanctions

To ensure that the ARGA does enforce rules speedily (rather than the FRC's older investigations, which went on for year), there should be temporary sanctions whilst the full investigation occurs. Temporary fines in the form of withholding salaries or claiming back bonuses should be enforceable during this process. Banning from working temporarily should also be possible. To ensure that ARGA acts quickly, they would be subject to ARGA and select committee interrogation and also, if necessary, direct action by the Business Minister. The select committee chairperson should be able to make recommendations (publicly) to the Department of Business if he or she feels ARGA is not taking action quickly enough or is not levying temporary fines and/or exclusions. Board members who are not members of a professional accounting body could still be fined or temporarily banned from being a director.

3) Pension payments and dividends

We would like to see the possibility of ARGA fining members of the board if dividends are paid in preference to pension contributions without good and justifiable reasons. This is not an all or nothing issue, just that dividends and pension gaps should be made in some sort of proportion. Dividends should not be paid if no contribution to any pension's gap is being made. For example, Carillion continued to pay dividends without closing the pensions gap, as shown in the case study of Carillion in Chapter 6 of Volume 2: *Financial Failures & Scandals: From Enron to Carillion.*[6] This should be part of the FRC/ARGA guidance and perhaps necessitates a change in law.

4) Comprehensive income report

Mandatory standardised and audited comprehensive income report.

5) Off-balance sheet items

An audited statement of all off-balance sheet items without exception.

The short-term remedies on the balance sheet

6) Multiple balance sheets

Discussions between Krish Bhaskar and Rod Sellers led to this possible solution – involving the concept of an average balance sheet based on three balance sheets i.e. opening and closing balance sheets (audited as per normal) and one interim balance sheet during the year, probably after six months and with more disclosures than in the current interim financial statements.

If there are any special circumstances that change during the period, then these should be clearly stated with a closing like-for-like balance sheet and then the closing balance sheet with the changes (for example, a rights issue or major acquisition and/or with significant changes in goodwill).

The opening and closing balance sheets are a given and audited. We would like the intermediate balance sheet(s) to be audited/reviewed as well. Even if they are not, there is some merit to providing the average of all of the balance sheets alongside the closing balance sheet and prior years' of both (preferably for three years).

Short-term remedies on length of report including brevity, comprehensibility, meaningfulness

7) Separating reports

Over time, an expanded number of standardised reports may be set by e.g. standard-setting bodies and the ARGA, but integrated reports may be abandoned gradually over time (as is happening already).

8) Sustainability

Separate the sustainability element in to a separate report – as many companies already do – with a one-page summary in the main report.

9) Remuneration

One-page summary with the detail as a separate remuneration report.

The basic idea here is that there are multiple reports geared to the needs of different classes of users and stakeholders. Muddy Waters Research fund (head: Carson Block) may want to plough through pages of remuneration of directors to see what bonus payments have been paid and why. However, most users will just want to see the overall scale of remuneration and not dwell on the detail. Both should be available. Hence the CORE and MORE approach outlined in Chapter 4 or what we refer as hybrid reporting – multiple reports for different users. We return to the Kingman concept of 'brevity, comprehensibility, meaningfulness, and proportionality' later. We agree totally with this type of paradigm.

Short-term remedies on survival (going concern, viability, and resilience)

10) Better neutrality on narrative sections
The FRC decided to strengthen the going-concern statement (affecting external auditors).[7] The Brydon review[8] made the suggestion to replace the going-concern and viability statements with a resilience report. See Appendix 3.07.2 for further details. We argue that a longer-term solution is to have a numerical forecast with sensitivity analysis stress testing.

11) Audit of the whole report including narrative sections
This quick fix is to adopt the suggestion of Stephen Haddrill, ex-chief executive of the FRC, to expand auditors' responsibilities, by requiring them to examine companies' financial reports from 'front to back'. Nigel Sleigh-Johnson, head of the financial reporting faculty at ICAEW,[9] said, 'It is entirely possible for an auditor to give an opinion over the whole of an annual report'. This would be a quick fix but not wholly satisfactory. We consider another alternative below. Kingman also supports the whole report being audited, and so do we.

However, there are issues to be decided. Words are imprecise, debatable, and ambiguous. We believe that there is a need for some sort of neutral independent review/report on the narrative sections of the annual report – not undertaken by the auditors. The problem remains that auditors are not independent enough, and words are imprecise.

In the first instance, this could be an external auditor and was discussed by the FRC/ARGA/Kingman review.[10] Aberdeen Standard Investments support this concept. GT (Grant Thornton, one of the smaller challenger firms to the Big Four) is against, but if it means higher audit fees (which we think are low in any case) then that will cover the additional cost and overcome any practicalities.[11] The three authors support the greater neutrality for the narrative text – though we are happy that simulacra are left in, and each advocates a slightly different approach. See Appendix 3.07.3 to see our longer-term suggestions on narrative solutions in the audit process.

12) Numerical forecast

Forecasts for several years including at least three previous years' forecasts versus actuals (where available) should be provided. These should include, at the minimum, a simplified cash-flow forecast and a profit forecast. Additional audit/assurance fees for this aspect could be charged. To preserve proportionality a set of the largest or most important large private companies would have to undertake the same hurdle. Adding non-listed companies is a departure from the current norm.

Bhaskar and John Flower would like the forecast period to be for the current year and 5 future years. Sellers argues for only 3 years. He feels that forecasts should be meaningful rather than an accountants' extrapolation of figures. Senior management and the chief executive should buy into the forecast. There should be a reconciliation each year of actuals against forecasts. Also, a profit forecast for the current year should be published on the company's website (to be included in the annual report).

The measure of profit should be net income before tax including all exceptional and non-recurring items, an operating profit figure, an underlying operating profit, and perhaps an EBITDA. It may be appropriate for the forecast to be summarised in the annual report and for there to be documented change control and for the details to be available on the firm's website. If the website profit forecast is changed, then the reason and data for that change plus the previous profit forecast for the last 12 months should be shown alongside.

13) Signing off the report and website information

The chief executive should sign off by name the above forecasts in the annual report and any accounting information, metrics, or reports on their website.

Short-term remedies for the TPR and BEIS Insolvency service

14) The Pensions Regulator (TPR)

TPR insists on trustees for defined benefit pension schemes where the trustees have various duties to perform.[12] Guidance for these trustees is comprehensive.[13] The trustee has to examine forecasts that show sufficient financial resources to fund pensions or any shortfall. If the pensions' trustees are satisfied with their review, then this should be stated and signed by the named trustee in the report.

15) The Insolvency Service

This service coupled with the Department of Business (BEIS) should have a special division to investigate the closures of companies and also in some extreme cases company voluntary arrangements (CVA) – as is occurring with restaurants chains and high street retail outlets/chains/stores in 2020 hastened by the pandemic. They may refer to FRC/ARGA for disciplinary action as well if this body has powers as in quick-fix point number 1 (penalties on management). If not, this unit should have fining and exclusion powers on non-accountant individuals (BEIS already has exclusion powers for company directors, but this is weak and is rarely used and needs to be beefed up).

Short-term remedies on the ability of professional investors and hedge funds/shorters gaining privileged information – dissemination of information from management to certain classes of investors

Despite horrific penalties for inside trading, the evidence shows that certain, often privileged classes of professional investors and fund managers do regard informal, off-the-record meetings with management as the most important source of information – not necessarily published information available to all. So this may not be insider trading, but it is certainly fairly close, and regardless of whether it actually influences share purchase/hold/sale decisions, we think the playing field should be levelled.

16) Management meetings with report users to be available

All meetings, however informal, to be recorded and a summary published on the firm's website, including meetings over lunch but within reason (bumping into someone on the way to a station may not count).

17) Management presentations

All (without exception and even informal and off-the-record) analyses and other presentations by management to be shown on the website except for presentations to bankers, investment banks, or anyone seriously providing finance, and in connection with share issues, loans, any sort of borrowing or mortgages, and leases. In the latter case, sensitive information could be redacted.

Short-term remedies for private companies to avoid BHS-type events

The BHS scandal is covered and discussed in the book Volume 2: *Financial Failures & Scandals: From Enron to Carillion.*[14] BHS was sold by Sir Philip Green for next to nothing but had substantial pension liabilities. BHS then failed, leaving a substantial pension shortfall close to £700 million (and perhaps more). In the end, Sir Philip made a voluntary contribution for some of this shortfall (around £363 million).

18) Extension to private companies

To avoid the sort of issues found with BHS, we would like to see all such large private companies brought into the reporting and auditing framework of listed FSTE 100 companies. Adding private/non-listed companies is a departure from the current norm. Appendix 3.07.4 has a list of large private companies which should produce the full PIE report. However, there are others, and we think a threshold revenue of £100 million and more than 1,000 employees should be included. These include Frasers Group (formerly Sports Direct), John Lewis, Swire, JCB, Arcadia, Virgin Atlantic, Iceland, and more than 100 others. Krish Bhaskar did make several written recommendations to the various reviews over the years, but they were all ignored.

One of the problems of private companies is that they often hide their principle company away or under different names. Cambridge Analytica[15] is an example, where the real business is conducted under the name SCL, with a host of companies (at least seven UK and many more overseas), each of which owes other companies money and some of which have bought one another – also Ember Data, Firecrest Technologies, which look as if they may continue after the closure of the other companies.[16] There are also subsidiaries in the US, Romania, Canada, and a few other countries.

Another is the famous JCB manufacturer. There are many companies listed with the JCB name. The actual master consolidated accounts are under the name JCB Service. JCB also has substantial overseas operations in India – which are consolidated into the UK company accounts – but the extent to which the overseas operations will be consolidated in the future may be in doubt. Dyson is now under Weybourne Group, where the HQ/holding company is located in Singapore.

Trying to fathom the totality of these linked companies under common management will always be difficult. Some sort of order needs to be brought to such private companies (which includes companies with multiple defence contracts). Similarly, Cambridge Analytica used confidential Facebook data for political purposes. The set of companies allied to Cambridge Analytica had a combined turnover of well over £100 million for 2016 (we estimate).

Short-term remedy on comparative historical data

19) Mandatory financial history

Six-year or 10-year history of income statement and balance sheets even if in simplified form, all to be stated using the same valuation methods and with notes under each year showing any major changes due to expansion or contraction, acquisitions and/or mergers, or disposals.

20) Non-financial information

Should include a range of (to be agreed) standard and industry standard APMs and KPIs.

Short-term remedy for whistleblowers

21) Protection for whistleblowers

They are an important source when management or others attempt to deliberately do something wrong – whether fraud or manipulation of the financial statements – so some action that causes someone some financial harm. We think it regrettable that Barclays Bank's chief executive, Jes Staley, was able to use the full power of his position and Barclay's resources to uncover a whistleblower about a senior appointment. Jes Staley was reprimanded and fined (sum undisclosed) by the FCA and the PRA (Prudential Regulation Authority [for banks]) – though his salary was £3.9 million with a bonus of more than £1 million in 2017 (he has a right of appeal, which is pending).[17]

The point is that the watchdogs (FRC/ARGA, FCA, PRA, and TPR) should have some power to protect and safeguard a whistleblower. For a chief executive of many FTSE 100 companies, a fine of £1 million would not be a significant burden. So far, the watchdogs have been reluctant to even reprimand let alone fine chief executives. Wirecard is another example.

Short-term remedy on sectors that are suffering
from severe disruption

22) Different information for businesses facing different risks

Most retail outlets are suffering from the switch to online, plus changing demographics and shopping patterns, and in many towns, the effects
of austerity are still present. The pandemic may also cause similar or
accelerated changes.

Burnley-based retailer The Original Factory is a retailer that has had to
put together a rescue package.[18] This outlet is actually owned by Duke
Street Capital. (That and the shop only have dormant accounts, so we
cannot check.) The point is that many of such retailers will have had
to report on their strategy and risks. Many of them will know they are
suffering a systemic decline in revenues. Somehow, we do not think
that they will always be that truthful in their annual report and financial statements. Often, the external auditors will sign off the business
as a going concern when it might not be that straightforward. Rescue
packages and company voluntary arrangements (CVAs) with debtors
are now commonplace.

We think that all retailers without a growing, stable, and viable online
business should give some sort of health warning about the disrupting
effects of online businesses. That health warning should be echoed by the
external auditors in terms of a comment on going concern and viability.
The same might apply to businesses that might be affected by Brexit or
changes due to the coronavirus pandemic.

If a retailer signs a lease agreement and then argues for a CVA, if there
was a health warning in the accounts, the property owner might have no
right of claim. But if there was no health warning in their accounts, then
we think a CVA should be questionable in the courts. The law may need to
be changed to accommodate this change – both in the annual report and to
the law governing CVAs. This would allow the landlords so affected (many
now) to be able to take out some sort of insurance or to come to some compensation arrangement with the retailer.

COVID-19 and its aftermath should also have a special financial health
warning. The K-shaped recovery looks as if some segments of the economy
have recovered sharply, while others have continued to downtrend. Those
in a downward spiral need to be able to warn all stakeholders of the impact
of COVID-19.

See Appendix 3.07.5 for a discussion on the question of proportionality.

Wirecard – suggestions arising out of this failure

23) Graded opinions for audit qualification

Graded opinions for audit qualification rather than the current, in effect, just pass or fail should be available. At the moment, there are mainly two outcomes:[19] unqualified or qualified. Or worse still, as in the case of Wirecard, the auditor EY (Ernst & Young [Germany]) refused to sign off the audit. Unqualified is assumed to mean a clean bill of health. Qualified is so rare that it might mean an immediate drop in share price (for a listed company) or difficulties in raising new loans or even maintaining existing loans. Certainly, it could indicate the collapse of the company, as indeed EY's failure to pass the accounts of Wirecard led to Wirecard's collapse.

Would it not be sensible at a time of extreme uncertainty to have an audit grading system – say 1 to 10 rather than just the pass/fail? No one predicted the coronavirus. And no one is going to be able to say how the future will hold for many sectors in the economy. Surely we need to bring the auditing stamp into this new 'normal' world. Whilst a qualified audit report or a failure to pass the accounts could cause, in effect, the demise of the company, a reduced grade would not cause the same havoc for an audited company.

Wirecard's problems arose much earlier with whistleblowers, hedge funds, and the FT warning of possible problems. This rose to a crescendo from 2015/16. KPMG conducted a special report handed over to Wirecard in April 2020. Then it was reported that EY could have provided an unqualified audit report when KPMG's special audit report (to allay rumours) had stunned investors after the firm was unable to verify the existence of half of the payment group's business. The FT report claims that EY may have demanded certain conditions to pass their accounts.[20]

This seems to smack of two concerns: Firstly, how could EY have countenanced providing an unqualified report given the number of rumours, whistleblowers, and the KPMG report? (Although EY now claim that they were responsible for exposing the fraud. Polite cough here.)

The second concern is although there are, in theory, four possible outcomes to an audit report (see endnote 19), in practice, it is pass or fail, unqualified or qualified. A finer granular system would provide better information and a more nuanced approach with less severe reactions (such as Wirecard's closure).

FRC's response

The FRC's Future of Corporate Reporting[21] essentially deals with the long term. The shorter terms issues were discussed in their regular annual review of reporting. Their 2019/20 review[22] concentrated on a few key aspects (apart from the new IFRS 15/16):

- Judgements and estimate: These should be tailored and relevant especially for the uncertainty embodied with the pandemic and Brexit.
- Impairment of assets – also impacted by the above. Specifically test the judgements on investments, tangible and intangible assets.
- Revenue from contracts with customers: The Rolls-Royce engine problem discussed in the next chapter. When revenue is recognised over time, rather than at a point in time, companies should explain the basis for selecting this accounting policy.
- Financial instruments: More information about liquidity risk in the current or risky circumstances.
- APMs: Users should be able to relate reconciling items to GAAP measures in the report and accounts.
- Strategic Report: Not always fair, balanced, and comprehensive view of the performance and position of the business.
- Statement of Cash Flows: The major source of restatements. Companies should also pay attention to: the classification of cash flows from unusual transactions, the inappropriate netting of gross cash flows and the disclosure of non-cash changes in financing liabilities.
- Provisions and Contingencies: Opaque and not transparent.
- Fair Value Measurement: Should be provided for all relevant areas of the financial statements, with explanations supporting judgements, and assumptions with sensitivity analyses where appropriate.
- Business Combinations: Companies should explain how acquired assets and liabilities, and any contingent consideration, are measured.

Where are we now?

These short-term remedies are a collection of changes that can produce better reporting during the next 3 to 5 years. However, there are longer-term changes: a move away from profit maximising; the valuation issues of intangibles; companies where the market capitalisation has no bearing to book value; and so on. These we now examined in the last two chapters together with what we regard as more significant and fundamental changes.

Notes

1 Kingman Report, Kingman report: Independent review of the financial reporting council, government, December 2018, available at: www.gov.uk/ government/publications/financial-reporting-council-review-2018, accessed December 2018.

2 Ibid.

3 K. Bhaskar and H. Flower, *Financial Failures & Scandals: From Enron to Carillion*, Vol. 2, Routledge, 2019, available at: www.amazon.co.uk/Financial-Failures-Scandals-Carillion-Disruptions/dp/0367220733/ref=sr_1_1?keywords= krish+bhaskar&qid=1565533613&s=gateway&sr=8-1.

4 Op. Cit. Kingman Report, 2018.

5 F. Wilkinson, From the top/restoring trust in audit, *Economia*, 17 July/ August 2019, available at: https://economia.icaew.com/opinion/july-2019/ restoring-trust-in-audit-fiona-wilkinson, accessed July 2019.

6 Op. Cit. Bhaskar and Flower, 2019.

7 FRC, FRC strengthens going concern audit standard, *FRC News*, 30 September 2019, available at: www.frc.org.uk/news/september-2019/frc-strengthens-going-concern-audit-standard, accessed June 2020.

    The new standard can be accessed at: www.frc.org.uk/getattachment/13b19 e6c-4d2c-425e-84f9-da8b6c1a19c9/ISA-UK-570-revised-September-2019-Full-Covers.pdf and several additions in December 2020 https://www.frc.org. uk/news/december-2020/frc-highlights-importance-of-a-challenge-culture-i https://www.frc.org.uk/news/december-2020/frc-announces-its-thematic-reviews,-audit-areas-of https://www.frc.org.uk/news/december-2020/new-research-supports-introduction-of-standards-fo though the audit firms are responding with enhanced measures to form their evaluation of companies' going concern assessments: https://www.frc.org.uk/news/november-2020/ audit-firms-enhance-going-concern-assessments.

8 D. Brydon, Assess, assure and inform. Improving audit quality and effectiveness. Report of the independent review into the quality and effectiveness of audit, December 2019, pages 80–82, pages 10 and 80–82, available at, https://assets. publishing.service.gov.uk/government/uploads/system/uploads/attachment_ data/file/852960/brydon-review-final-report.pdf, accessed December 2019.

9 https://economia.icaew.com/en/news/april-2018/frc-seeks-to-expand-auditors-responsibilities

10 Op. Cit. Kingman Report, 2018.

11 M. Marriage, Accounting watchdog eyes 'front-to-back' audit of annual reports, *Financial Times*, 4 April 2018, available at: www.ft.com/content/8f5ce606-375b-11e8-8b98-2f31af407cc8, accessed May 2018.

12 The Pensions Regulator website, available at: www.thepensionsregulator.gov. uk/trustees.aspx.

13 The Pensions Regulator website, available at: www.thepensionsregulator.gov. uk/guidance/guidance-for-trustees.aspx#s23610.

14 Op. Cit. Bhaskar and Flower, 2019.

15 Cambridge Analytica was a British political consulting firm that combined misappropriation of digital assets and violated privacy using Facebook data.

16 Firecrest dissolved, but Ember Data was still trading in 2020.

17 P. Collinson and Agency, Barclays CEO Jes Staley faces fine over whistleblower incident, *The Guardian*, 20 April 2018, available at: www.theguardian.com/

business/2018/apr/20/barclays-ceo-jes-staley-facing-fine-over-whistleblower-incident, accessed May 2018.

18 M. Ribbeck, Burnley-based bargain store is putting together rescue package, *The Business Desk*, 30 April 2018, available at: www.thebusinessdesk.com/north-west/news/2020308-burnley-based-bargain-store-latest-retailer-hit-problems, accessed May 2018.

19 In reality, there are four types of opinion: unqualified opinion – clean report; qualified opinion – qualified report; disclaimer of opinion – disclaimer report; and adverse opinion – adverse audit report. But they are rarely used. It is a question of an audit opinion (unqualified) or one qualified.

20 O. Storbeck, EY prepared unqualified audit for Wirecard in early June, *Financial Times*, 23 July 2020, available at: www.ft.com/content/568d5f9f-ebbe-48fc-a7b7-0ebf34c3cb83, accessed July 2020.

21 FRC, The future of corporate reporting discussion paper, *FRC News*, 8 October 2020, available at: https://www.frc.org.uk/news/october-2020/frc-publishes-future-of-corporate-reporting-discus, accessed October 2020.

22 FRC, Annual Review of Corporate Reporting 2019/20, *FRC News*, 202, available at: https://www.frc.org.uk/accountants/corporate-reporting-review/annual-review-of-corporate-reporting, accessed October 2020.

8   Conflicting objectives in financial reporting

Conflicting objectives of reports

Maximising profits, maximising shareholder value – such concepts make for neat theoretical economic and financial models that are easy to manipulate and obtain solutions. However, they are too simplistic for real life firms. Many of the recent developments in financial and corporate reporting can best be explained as the outcome of a struggle between the proponents of different concepts of the function of the annual report. That said, internal reporting systems can be incorrect, misleading, manipulated, or inadequate (*à la* Carillion, Patisserie Valerie, and others).

For most readers of annual reports, the remuneration report is glossed over. The detailed directors' remuneration report was an average of 19 pages long for the FTSE 100 (in 2017). These reports are usually in small font/print and in triple columns. They are probably only going to be studied in detail by a handful of professional investors. Occasionally, there may be a shareholder revolt on remuneration (discussed in the next section). However, in normal times, the remuneration report goes unread except by the few analysts or a block of shareholders who feel executive pay is too much. The majority of readers or users of annual reports want other information from the report.

John Flower, in his book on *Accounting and Distributive Justice*, had already identified the need for differing functions (distribution, reporting, and information), But he also noted that 'different stakeholders have different information needs and that, therefore, it is appropriate to provide them with different types of information'.[1]

Shareholders versus stakeholders versus directors

There is a struggle that has influenced the reporting requirements of companies: that of shareholders versus directors. This reflects the basic conflict between ownership and control that was identified by Berle and Means[2] more than 80 years ago. Essentially, the regulators, responding to pressure from shareholders and their representatives, have sought to strengthen the position of shareholders vis-à-vis directors. Typical pressure points include:

a   Directors' remuneration: Persimmon has been in the news in recent years with an original pay award for the then-CEO (Jeff Fairburn) of £100 million in 2018. Google's Alphabet CEO (Sundar Pichai) was paid $280 million for 2019. Most of these pay awards occur because the value of their shares increase, and this may have nothing to do with the actual performance of the company. Other revolts of this nature include Vistry, Morrisons, Tesco, Virgin Money, Ryanair, Redrow, JD Sports, Pearson, British Airways, Plus500, Ted Baker, and Boohoo, among others, in 2020.

b   Auditors: The appointment of an auditor where there has been issues with the a company's accounts. GE had an issue in the US with shareholders over the reappointment of KPMG after several accounting issues concerning valuations. In the UK, a similar shareholder protest incurred over the appointment of PwC for British Telecom after a damaging scandal at its Italian business in which a fraud went undetected – though KPMG were already announced to replace PwC.

c   Strategy: This is usually precipitated by activist shareholders such as forcing Whitbread to sell off Costa Coffee before management were willing to do so. In this case, Elliott Advisors had built up a stake in Whitbread of more than 6%. The most famous minority shareholder row concerns Sir Stelios Haji-Ioannou (holding 34% of EasyJet's shares). He most recently (2020) wanted to remove the four directors in a special shareholder vote and cancel a £4.5 billion order for more than 100 new aircraft from Airbus, which he believed put the future of the airline in doubt but he has often had many earlier disputes with the board.

Conflicting aspirations for the annual report

The FRC, over the last few years (since around 2014), has led to the expansion of the front half of the annual report (the narrative sections). Gender and supply chain payments information have been added via a government website. The FRC and its replacement ARGA are still pushing for more information to be disclosed in the annual report. These changes are just a wider part of the push for greater reporting – and the annual report as a main plank of reporting is expanding and will continue to adapt and change. The pandemic of 2020 will lead to a greater emphasis on possible risks, however unlikely.

Many of the recent developments in financial and corporate reporting can best be explained as the outcome of a struggle between the proponents of different concepts of the function of the annual report. The theoretical model, as stated before, is that the company is run by management for the benefit of shareholders. However, shareholders show few signs of interfering with management. For example, an article by David Cumming, who is chief investment officer for equities at Aviva Investors, makes the case that institutional shareholders are more or less not engaged enough.[3] He argues that institutional shareholders need to be as agile and active as private equity in dealing with failures of leadership.

Private equity's growth at the expense of listed companies was discussed in Chapter 3. This is often to escape the rigours of reporting regulations on listed companies or short-term pressure from shareholder groups, their proxies, or hedge funds. One of the negative events associated with private equity is when private equity firms buy listed companies, saddling them with debt to repay the private equity firm for the investment; such leveraged buyouts are discussed in Appendix 3.08.1. Such leveraged buyouts can lead to problems when a downturn comes or revenues dip. Other negative effects include asset stripping and too much aggressive cost cutting.

Recently, the FT documented several negative views on the growth of private equity in the face of private equity bids for G4S. (Finally the company was bought by a US rival, Allied Universal Security Service, for £3.8 billion). Other targets included Cobham, McCarthy & Stone, AA, Countrywide, and others, with the global buyout private equity having amassed around $2.5 trillion (as at the beginning of 2021).[4] Phone4U and Debenhams are two examples often used to argue against private equity. The alternative positive view is that it allows firms to take a longer-term view.

However, it is obvious that the institutional shareholders, their proxies, and the NEDs are often painfully unaware of their duties or too lazy or just negligent. Proxy advisory firms and hedge funds have taken a much more active role of late, though not always. This and other conflicting goals are also explored in Appendix 3.08.2 dealing with conflicting objectives of reports.

The growth of other objectives apart from shareholders' wealth

So where are we? Financial reporting and the wider corporate reporting originated in a way to account for stewardship to the owners, the shareholders. The Western markets adopted the single objective of the firm as profit maximising – maximising the value of shareholders wealth which, once interest rates are taken into account, implies maximising the net present value of the stream of dividends and other cash streams to and from the shareholders. The Japanese and some Asian markets (not so much Hong Kong and Singapore) interpreted their fundamental objective as long-term growth. Of course, Trumpian economics with the corporate tax cuts has led to money being returned to shareholders and/or a buyback of the firms' own shares. It is not just dividends that are the only cash stream to and from shareholders.

For some time, the environmental lobby has been growing (with justification) to measure the environmental impact of firms. More recently, the collapse of Carillion and Patisserie Valerie has demonstrated that employees interests should not be ignored. And the Carillion collapse caused inconvenience to the government. The switch from brick-and-mortar stores to online retailing has led to upwards of many thousands of stores closing each year and has underlined the importance of employment opportunities. The 2020 pandemic just heightened this switch.

The multiple objectives are being reported more widely:[5]

> A group of influential investors, academics and lawyers is pushing for big companies to publicly declare how they will 'profitably achieve a solution for society' after a major US business group unexpectedly dropped its creed of shareholder primacy.
>
> The initiative, led by Oxford university's Saïd Business School, Berkeley law school and Hermes EOS – the investment manager's engagement and stewardship division – wants company directors to provide a one-page 'statement of purpose', detailing the most important stakeholders and time frames for evaluating strategy and how capital is spent.
>
> Their aim is to counter what they call the 'misconception' that directors' only fiduciary duty is to shareholders.

Multiple objectives are being heralded in the US despite former President Trump's drive to roll back corporate regulations:[6]

> One of America's largest business groups has dropped the 'shareholder primacy' creed that has driven US capitalism for decades, urging companies to consider the environment and workers' wellbeing alongside their pursuit of profits.
>
> The Business Roundtable (BRT) has close to 200 members, including the chief executives of JPMorgan, Amazon and General Motors, which generate $7tn in annual revenue. A new 'statement of purpose' from the BRT on Monday placed shareholders as one of five stakeholders, alongside customers, workers, suppliers and communities.
>
> It is a significant departure from the bedrock belief that businesses serve the owners of their capital – a philosophy championed by Nobel Prize–winning economist Milton Friedman and which has driven corporate America for decades.

Companies should 'protect the environment' and treat workers with 'dignity and respect' while also delivering long-term profits for shareholders, the BRT said.

The change amounts to a call to reform capitalism in a time in which rising populism and concern about climate change have led politicians and shareholder activists to demand that companies consider their impact on the world beyond their balance sheets.

This indicates, we believe, that there are at least several other objectives being pursued as of 2020.

Reporting and objectives in the long term

Who are the reports for?

Who will be the user in the 2030 time frame? We do not expect to see much change, just a gradual move to a longer-term position and a wider set of stakeholders – not just the investors.

By the 2030-to-2050 time frame? The quick answer is everybody. Stakeholders will have progressively widened. Employees, the supply chain, and debtors and creditors, including customer and the state, will be given a much higher priority in their reporting needs and the information tailored to what each group may be interested in. In Appendix 3.08.3, mainly drawn from John Flower's earlier work, we consider the theory of who might actually use the reports – the possible stakeholders.

The assumptions dominating our time frame of a longer-term horizon include a very different set of reporting requirements by a wider set of users/readers/stakeholders and a much more demanding public. We believe that public perceptions will be augmented by a more open society and much greater transparency – even far past the point of hiding information from competitors. That, we imagine, would not be a concern in such a society. So the list of who might or will use the financial and corporate reports becomes much larger. Reporting may develop in the form of one integrated report or, more likely, the hybrid approach split into CORE and a number of MORE or smaller narrower reports. Some (including one senior Big Four colleague) advocate that even just sheer data may be sufficient, structured or raw, together with artificial intelligence tools to make sense or to pull the relevant parts for any query or user view.

As a whole, we have to assume that the set of users is just about everybody when you take into account current as well as potential users. The delivery system for reports may be very different – sometimes produced for the user by their AI assistant, sometimes digested by media, social media, and relevant blogs. In addition, the method of delivery of the reports will be different. The major delivery method of general and bespoke news will be via some sort of AI-assisted reporting system. Even if it is not, the information will be delivered to your smart watch/pen, your glasses, your wearable, or, just possibly, that old-fashioned but much-enhanced smart phone now dominated by just a few players such as: Samsung, Apple/iPhone, Huawei, Xiaomi, and the manufacturers of Google/Pixel[7], and a combination of Oppo/Vivo/Xiaomi/LG.Motorola/Mobicel/Lenovo/Nokia. In addition, of course, the information could be delivered directly to one's mind (via Elon Musk's Neuralink).

How and to what extent should companies meet the demands of diverse stakeholder groups?

Resetting capitalism: demise of the current capitalist model

The current (liberal) capitalist model is undergoing change. In the decade since the GFC, the model has come under strain, especially the underlying theoretical assumption on maximising profits and shareholder value. The FT, in a series, of articles[8] questioned the perceived profit/shareholder-value maximising model. These articles[9,10,11] made the case for substantially modifying this model to include the state, a wider set of stakeholders (customers and suppliers), and all citizens (affected by an impact of externalities). The FT argued:[12]

> The long-term health of free enterprise capitalism will depend on delivering profit with purpose. Companies will come to understand that this combination serves their self-interest as well as their customers and employees.

Without change, the prescription risks being far more painful.

This initiative formed a major focus on the newspaper and on the website pages of the FT: https://aboutus.ft.com/en-gb/new-agenda/. The thesis of the FT editorial is that the long-term health of free-enterprise capitalism will depend on delivering profit with multiple purposes/goals. Companies will come to understand that a combination of objectives serves their self-interest as well as their customers and employees.[13,14,15,16]

Multiple objectives, uses, and values in the long term

Disruption to traditional valuation models

Then think about Apple. Net income is after tax of close to $60 plus billion with revenues in excess of $260 billion a year (tax is low being an arrangement with its HQ in Ireland. Apple's low tax payments is due to agreed arrangement between the company and the tax authorities in Ireland for having its HQ there (but contested by the EU).[17] The company has a balance sheet total of well under $400 billion, with $200 billion being cash or near cash, and a market capitalisation of well over $1 trillion (in 2019, cash dropped a little in 2020). Apple is joined by Amazon, Microsoft, Facebook, and Alphabet/Google with market capitalisations of more than $1 trillion. Then think of high-share-value firms still making losses (as of 2020): Uber, Lyft, Pinterest, Snapchat, GE, even Tesla at one earlier point. Nikola Corp (a zero-emission/electric truck and lorry manufacturer), in June 2020, the company's market capitalisation briefly over-took Ford's despite not producing one vehicle – production (if at all) may take place in 2022. Recent high value but loss making companies include Airbnb and Slack. All these are dominated by US firms.

What is the relevance of our conventional financial statements? Answer: very little. In the case of new tech companies, it may be that the number of active subscribers is a much more relevant statistic.

Mario Abela, a director of the World Business Council for Sustainable Development and a visiting professor at the IESEG (Institut d'Economie Scientifique et de Gestion) business school in Paris, goes on to argue that business models are diverging. For example, Rolls Royce makes money out of its jet engines by charging customers on a fixed cost-per-flying-hour basis. Netflix and Amazon Prime both have a subscription model. Then there is the on-demand online business model of Uber, Airbnb, and Deliveroo. Then again, Google, Facebook, and Twitter gain value from letting us use their services free of charge, though they can generate value through our actions. Their motivation is that they can then sell that information on users to advertisers, who then target adverts to us.

Multiple objectives, goals, and constraints

The single objective of profit or wealth maximisation may be replaced by a more flexible range of multiple goals and constraints. Goals are clear objectives for what you want your end state to be, while constraints are given conditions or circumstances that your solution must satisfy. In this context, a constraint has to be met. After meeting those constraints, one can then manoeuvre and push towards goals while still meeting those constraints – something Krish Bhaskar learnt in his research work on goal programming. Constraints are hard points (to be exactly met); then the system optimises its given goals after meeting any constraints. But constraints might be goals but just have to be exactly met – not less nor more. A goal that needs to be flexible and then optimised is the residual goal and not a constraint. Of course, this is too simplistic. There may be a multitude of flexible criteria whilst not being hard constraints, but some may have higher priorities than others.

Let us illustrate this with The Crown Estate, one of the first entities to use integrated reporting. It is an independent commercial business, created by an Act of Parliament but belonging to the British monarch. It invests in and manages some of the UK's most important assets, aiming to create significant value beyond financial return. Actually, it is required to follow the profit motive. However, one could imagine that such a semi-royal organisation which looks after the coastline and has large chunks of farmland and property, would be an ideal organisation to have a variety of objectives. It already says that its business model is distinctive, combining business with stewardship. Of course, the concept of stewardship can mean many different things. Remember that 58% of the entity's property value is in London (including the entire freehold of Regent Street in London) and about half the coastline. Here is what a multiple-objective approach might evolve into:

Hard constraints to be met:

Minimum financial earnings and earnings for the UK government treasury

Maintenance to a specified standard of the coastline and Windsor estates, etc.

Any other royal requirements

Goals and objectives to be maximised with differing priorities:

To be a good and fair landlord

Environmental goals in specified terms of CO_2, NO_x, and carbon

Aesthetic aims – leaving the landscapes under their control as beautiful as possible.

In general, looking forward a decade or two, the profit-maximising or shareholder-maximising paradigm will become old hat. It will be replaced by a number of considerations. Profits and dividends will be more of a constraint. There may be leverage and working-capital constraints. Supplier treatment and customer satisfaction may become goals or constraints in their own right. Employee satisfaction will probably be a major hard constraint. Growth considerations (organic or acquisitions) are for the long term and are flexible goals.

So we can envisage a commercial world in which any large company will have a number of objectives and constraints. Each organisation might be different. The focus may be on the short term or the long term, but it should be stated. The organic growth versus takeover expansion or contraction should be clearly outlined.

Now how is this relevant to reporting?

Business models and the preparers offering multiple valuation models

The conventional view of profit maximising or wealth creation for shareholders is being challenged in many quarters, including, as we have seen, public perceptions and the upcoming new generations of the UK, US, and European population cohorts, who show a rising interest in a wider set of personal goals. This is coupled with what might be regarded as the failure of capital markets and the new growth of financing by new non-legacy forms, including crowdfunding.

Even the ICAEW and also the FEE[18] already have referred to this widening of objectives. So there is much disagreement with the importance of the investors' view; these other interests could claim that their 'capital' is just as much at risk as that of investors. Suppliers, for example, might claim that they provide credit, which is a form of financial capital. So would customers paying in advance. Employees invest 'human capital' and financing capital (as they are paid at the end of a period) in a company and bear risk in their future livelihoods, the risk of redundancies and uncertainties in pension values, and even the existence of a pension (as the BHS and Arcadia retailer incidents have shown). Some might say that the contribution these stakeholders make to value creation entitles them to relevant information from the business.

However, it goes wider than this. The objectives in reporting also depend on what society currently demands of reporting. The perceptions gap has to close in the future. The narrow view of servicing investors or the capital markets will be heavily modified in the future if not already. Carillion, Wirecard, and others all lend credence to that view. The government, society, suppliers, and employers all have rights (deemed by society) and have certain 'relevant' information. There may be a hierarchy of needs and levels of entitlement to information.

Alternative business models are developing, e.g. providing free services which provide value, on-demand services, and subscription-type services including the Rolls-Royce costs-per-hour for jet engines – a type of pay-as-you-use type model discussed in what follows. Alternative valuation rules can make large dramatic differences.

Take Rolls-Royce Holdings plc. This is the aerospace company (first formed in 1971 after the liquidation of the former company), which primarily sells jet engines. Their business model is to sell aero jet engines at a loss and recoup their profits through service and maintenance costs (the cost-per-hour), although they do not say this anywhere in their annual report, and their business model is boilerplate. This is their business model for aero engines. So traditionally, Rolls-Royce has always brought forward earnings from long-term service contracts – which make up roughly half of its revenue – to compensate for the fact that many aero engines are sold initially at a loss.

IFRS 15 (revenue recognition) determines when you can count revenues on a long-term contract. Rolls-Royce restated 2017 accounts showed a drop of £1.6 billion in revenue and a reduction in net profits of £825 million. The company is only allowed to recognise revenues when they are actually received. That is not representative of the business and does not provide an enduring realistic appraisal of profit, assuming the company continues in the same vein.[19] Of course, Carillion did the reverse by banking on revenues that never came. Each business is different.

While some argue IFRS 15 should lead to more appropriate accounting, Abela says a failure of financial reporting and the need for context force companies to turn to alternative performance measures and adjusted profits at the front of the annual report, 'because management believes the numbers don't reflect their business model'.[20] This raises our next topic: the objective of an organisation.

Rolls-Royce aero engines examples and reporting objectives

Assuming that we have powerful computer power and intelligent AIs to help, then any company could produce a set of accounts with US GAAP and IFRS accounts with and without mark-to-market and IFRS 15 revenue recognition. A company could present the firm's accounts in two separate ways. Rolls-Royce could add several versions showing different profit values depending on when they recognise revenue generation from their maintenance of jet engines. Of course, only one could be the official result, and whether these other versions are audited is something that needs to be considered – we think probably yes (the underlying accounts having been verified once, the additional cost may not be too great). It is possible that they may be audited – all of them. However, if not, it is the board's responsibility, and we assume that in the future, the board/management can be fined and/or be banned from a directorship if they fudge the results unacceptably.

So we can conceive of a financial reporting system, as modified by our short-term remedies but with multiple valuation methods. Management, in this case, wants to show the company as best it can using an appropriate valuation method which suits the circumstances of the company. Selling engines at low prices and possibly at a loss then recouping profits by a longer stream of profitable maintenance revenues is a valid business model. With the external auditors' permission and consent and with a justification by the firm and supported by the external auditors, this could be achieved in the CORE report, where there would be an IFRS set of financial statements and then an alternative set of statements with a valuation framework that was more appropriate for the Rolls-Royce model (assuming it continued in business). Both sets would need to be audited, and Rolls-Royce would have to pay for the additional audit fees: two sets of accounts in the CORE report with brief reconciliations and explanations; then a full and more detailed reconciliation and explanation in a MORE report. Even more alternative financial statements, valuation, and accounting standards could be added in a MORE report.

The external auditors' permission and consent are vital to stop choosing and manipulating the results just because it might show the highest profit value. In the event of a different valuation method chosen in parallel, the firm and auditors should provide some stress tests. These are discussed later.

Other business models and reporting objectives

Similarly, ride-hailing firm Uber has large initial outlays for autonomous taxis, on-demand services have the high launch cost of website development (which is their operation), and Google, Facebook, etc. had vast expenditure up front without any profit for years. Amazon has struggled with profitability for years and only in 2015 turned the corner, with substantial profits being generated from 2018 onwards – Jeff Bezos ploughed any cash generated back into further expansion for years.

Subscription models generate revenue in later years. Of course, some of these subscription type models suffer from acquisition and then retention issues – acquiring subscribers may be costly, and then they may leave for another service (loyalty not being a strong point among subscription services).

Reporting objectives where we need to stretch immediate profits into the future

Telecom companies, software suppliers, and any business that issues licences to use its products are among those most likely to be affected. They receive money early and up front and then have a stream of expenditure to provide the services for which people paid the licence fee. IFRS 15 will force companies to match revenues more closely to the work that is performed to earn them. In such companies, this could mean profits are booked earlier, which could cause challenges in later years.

Business models where the users want multiple valuation models

Do investors assess financial reporting information differently depending on whether they wish to judge the various aspects of a company? Some investors want growth. The shareholders of Carillion might have been happier with just stewardship – keeping the assets of the company intact. Others, as we found with our interviews, choose a Mike Ashley management style, and Sports Direct (now Frasers Group) has performed well for management performance and growth. Others wanted more safeguarding of assets with companies like AO (which, up to 2020, made a loss in every year) and Quindell. (Quindell did run into problems). Post-coronavirus survival may be most important. Assessment of risk, turning crises into opportunities, and such like may be the most valuable of management traits.

In general, we found that professional investors and institutional investors assess financial reporting information differently depending on their own objectives for their portfolio of shares. Some would want growth in share value; this would mean looking for high-tech companies early in their life or new on-demand services, though there is always risk with new services – one such is identified in Box 8.1. Others wanted a steady stream of earnings. Some were interested in short-term growth in share value, others in long-term growth. So how can we summarise these differing objectives of what investors may want from a set of financial statements?.

Box 8.1   The meal-kit service – risk with new on-demand services

For example, one of the growth on-demand (and sometimes subscription) services is that of meal kits, for which online websites deliver boxes of pre-portioned ingredients and easy-to-follow recipes to doorsteps. In the US, there are about 150 of such start-ups with a market that is valued at $2 billion; UK equivalents include Gousto, Mindfulchef, Riverford, and HelloFresh (also big in Germany). One of the largest is Blue Apron in the US, which has a subscription service for a fee of around $60 a week. Less than a year after it went public in June 2017 with a $1.9 billion valuation, Blue Apron has seen its share price fall by 80%. The reason is that shareholders are concerned that this type of service will fall prey to competition from big supermarkets. Albertsons, a US supermarket firm, bought a subscription-based meal-kit company and announced that meal kits would be available in hundreds of its stores in 2018. The giant Walmart group will soon do the same with its own kits in 2,000 of its stores. Amazon and Weight Watchers may be following shortly. In-store meal kits sidestep subscription-based services' problems of retention and acquisition.[21]

FRC Objective driven future of corporate reporting

Whilst the one set of principles advocated in the FRC proposals[22] seems sensible, it may be difficult to implement in practice and rather less transparent when applied to a specific business. Nevertheless most of the FRC observations we would agree with. There is one we find that our empirical research cannot verify and perhaps even the FRC's analysis is logically inconsistent. This concerns the objectives of reporting.

The FRC notes that the current framework for reporting focuses on the information needs of the primary users (often investors) and the provision of information through a single document: the annual report. This is now history.

The FRC believes that the objective of an individual network report should drive its content. This is a move away from the distinction between different user groups and their needs. We cannot agree. Different groups of users require different pieces of data to satisfy their curiosity or search (as in an encyclopedia rather than a novel [which is read from cover-to-cover]). The FRC evidence suggests that shareholder and other stakeholder expectations converge on many issues and that all users' needs are best served by structuring reporting around the purposes for which they seek information from a company. Our empirical evidence found the reverse – there is no convergence. For example, how many non-professional investors look through the detail of the remuneration report?

The FRC further considered a range of corporate reporting user groups and noted that the information needs of different user groups are not exclusive, and in many cases significantly overlap. We disagree – our evidence could not support this conclusion. The FRC also found that trying to establish distinguishing lines between different types of stakeholders and their information needs was unhelpful. We disagree. In the FRC's survey of financial reporting[23] the reason for low engagement with reporting items was for the most part 'The information is not relevant to me'.

However, the FRC in the same report acknowledges multiple objectives by proposing a corporate reporting model that provides for different communication objectives, including the FRC's proposal for a new Public Interest Report.

Critique of the FRC's Future of Corporate Reporting

The FRC, it will be remembered, postulated three central reports (financial statements, business report, and public interest report) plus four supporting reports (supporting detail, special purpose report, standing data, and other periodic reports). We agree with the overall approach (which accords with the main proposals in our book) but have certain reservations that are set out in the individual numbered questions below:

- The FRC's is arguing for three central reports and four ad-hoc reports. We think this is too restricted. There should be an opportunity to have one CORE report – broken down into the three sections as per the FRC suggestions and then to produce a number of supporting (the MORE) reports.

- The FRC's working assumption and their evidence suggests that share-holder and other stakeholder expectations converge on many issues and that all users' needs. As we have said we disagree. The empirical evidence we have collected supports our view is that different classes of stakeholders want (often radically) different information. The FRC seven reports structure could be augmented with additional reports and then our CORE and MORE comes close to the FRC suggestion.

- Implementation: A significant concern is the major increase in information to be published and the difficulty in assessing the value added for users compared with the cost to the company of gathering and presenting the information. Therefore we would propose that certain sections, especially the public interest report, are scaled back from your current proposals We think that size should not be the major determinate of whether this is included but the length of volume of such a report could provide proportionality.

- Non-financial information (NFI): The FRC highlight the need for "relevant, reliable, comparable and balanced information in the non-financial information section, which is laudable but, we believe, difficult to achieve. By its nature, non-financial information often involves high degrees of subjective views that cannot be "audited" with the same rigour as financial information. Indeed, by promoting these sections as equivalent to the financial information, they bestow an unworthy image of the factual basis for the statements.

- Regulatory standards for non-financial reporting: We believe regulatory standards are feasible for specific internal outcomes, for example, gender pay gap, length of credit taken from suppliers, modern slavery, etc. However for a multinational operating in a complex world of different cultures, geography and product markets, it may be meaningless to attempt to quantify what are, at best, averages – but averaging "apples and pears" is worthless. Perhaps separate meaningful reports for material subsections of the organisation would be better, although we respect that this goes against our previous plea to reduce the quantum of information to be published.

- Obligations in respect of the public interest: These can be overall expressions of a board's objectives but it may be difficult to substantiate that these fine sounding statements are rigorously applied at grass root levels

- Public Interest Report and the suggested content: Here we tend to prefer the more restrictive proposals from Brydon. If a company attempts to produce a Public Interest Report, it should be a standalone document giving the board's view of the external impacts of its operations. And the users can apply their own judgement on the value of the statements – otherwise we may find companies need to employ an army of "expert" consultants to vouch the board statements, a further expensive exercise with doubtful benefits.

• Another problem with quantifying external impacts is how far down the line from direct to indirect impacts should be referred to, for example, an oil company may be able to quantify the direct effects of an oil spillage in its exploration arm but it would be impossible to assess its external impacts from customers several stages down the line whose petrol driven cars produce emissions contributing to climate change, environment and public health.

Professional investors and the usefulness of financial reporting

Fortunately, we can draw upon a survey and detailed report by ICAS and EFRAG that came to some interesting conclusions.[24] Their report was based on both quantitative and qualitative data and evidence obtained from a series of 81 face-to-face interviews with professional investors based in 16 countries (but with the largest concentration of firms in the UK). In order to solicit investors' assessments of decision usefulness, the interviews were structured around a short fictional case containing abridged financial statement information on a large private European manufacturing firm that holds a significant portion of financial investments.

The principle take-away conclusion is that the objectives of users do matter. Re-interpreting their results, they conclude that financial reporting information is useful to professional investors overall. Several of our own interviews we have reported on claim that this is not true. However, when questioned, it was their reaction to the growing length of the annual report rather than the absence of any financial information.

We split this study into three objectives, though the original study identified just two: (a) valuation and (b) stewardship objectives. Disentangling the data and their results allowed us to add some of our own data and evidence. This allowed us to identify three broad objectives, though there was some overlap between them.

a   Performance of the management with an emphasis on short-term profitability. Professional investors are more likely to use information on cash flow forecasts or non-financial information. The focus may be on growth. An example of some analysts believing in management regardless are Mike Ashley and Sports Direct/Frasers Group. This conclusion is also supported by a *Harvard Business Review* study.[25]
b   Stewardship – here meaning the safeguarding and maintenance of assets; not losing money and paying a regular dividend. As well as the above traditional stewardship function – are the assets really there? These are the sort of questions thrown up by Wirecard, Steinhoff, Carillion, Patisserie Valerie, and others. Perhaps this is more important to those lending money

or who are in some way owed money or who are creditors. However, some professional shareholders who want steady dividends are also concerned with this aspect. For example, we found some analysts wary of Quindell on this criterion, and with hindsight, they may have been correct. Post-coronavirus, such objectives may once again come to the forefront.

c   Valuation of the company – growth in market capitalisation. This objective is for those professional investors who just want share value growth. Examples of companies that are based on valuation regardless of their financial results over time, Facebook, Amazon, Apple, Netflix, Google (or rather the holding company Alphabet) have grown their value massively from situations of reported losses or little profitability. The four firms are often known as the FANG or FAANG pack. The companies view profitability rather differently, too. Facebook and Google built enormous businesses first and are reinvesting the profits to develop new ones. All five (and other equivalent companies such as Tesla and, of course, Microsoft) continue to prioritise scale and have/are investing at the expense of profitability to achieve it. Historically, Facebook and Alphabet traded at a conservative 20 times earnings; the figure for Amazon and Netflix is closer to 100, and this is itself more than 5 times the average for members of the S&P 500. The companies still have important elements in common: dominance, scale, and growth. Each is at the top of its segment of the internet: Facebook in social media, Amazon in e-commerce, Netflix in premium video streaming, Google in search. All benefit from network effects, turbocharged by clever algorithms. The more users they have, the better their products, the more new customers are lured. This has helped them confound doubters and enabled them to grow briskly despite their massive size.[26]

Most of the examples for market capitalisation were given for the US. Leading UK companies were Autonomy (sold to HP), SwiftKey (acquired by Microsoft), TransferWise, possibly the accounting software company Sage, Shazam, Raspberry PI, ARM (sold to the Chinese Softbank Group in 2016 and bought by Nvidia in 2020), and others. Some of these such as Shazam have never made a profit but have 500 million subscribers and growing.

Added to the survey findings and their report, we have added our own findings and evidence to augment the ICAS results. Table 8.1 shows alternative measurement criteria broken down by the three different reporting objectives. (There may be more and with a more granular hierarchy of goals.)

In this table stakeholders who are interested in performance, stewardship or valuation might be classified by their possible likely constituents:

- Performance stakeholders: all possible classes of stakeholders
- Stewardship stakeholders: shareholders interested in a steady dividend flow, creditors, lenders, employees

Table 8.1 Measurement criteria versus different reporting objectives

	Performance of management	*Stewardship function, lenders*	*Valuation*
Function of the firm	Growth of the firm	Maintenance of the assets	To make money for the shareholders
Function of financial reporting	To report the economic performance of the firm	To report on safeguarding of the assets	To report the addition to wealth of the shareholders
How the firm's success is measured	EBITDA, revenue growth, NFI, comprehensive income	By tangible assets at historical cost and conservative value of intangibles	By the value of equity and any data that supports a higher valuation by the market
Important messages	Major changes in product or market share	Profit warnings, dividend payments	Profit warnings, dividend payments plus acquisitions
Primary financial statement	The income statement or P & L	The balance sheet	Both
Determination of income (profit)	Revenues less costs	Maintenance of value of the assets	Increase in market capitalisation, value of net assets
Nature of income (profit)	EBITDA, net profit	Both	Comprehensive income
Nature of a cost	An outlay recognised as a cost	Changes in assets value at historical cost or conservative valuation	A decrease in value of an asset
Nature of an asset	A resource of the firm	An outlay to be carried forward to be set against (matched with) future revenues	A resource of the firm
Measurement of assets or accounting valuation rules	Fair value	Historical cost	Current value
Revenue recognition	Optimistic	Conservative	Optimistic subject to valuation constraints
Theory of the firm	The entity theory: maximising profits or maximising growth opportunities	The proprietary theory	Maximising shareholder value

- Valuation stakeholders: Mainly shareholders, potential shareholders
- This table summarises our version of this study's findings, augmented by our own data. One interesting result from the survey data, which runs counter to press reports, is the importance of management remuneration. This survey showed that financial reporting information tied to managerial compensation has no significant effect on professional investors' assessments. Our data and evidence could not confirm that conclusion – often quite the reverse: sensible remuneration did matter for a small group of investors – who can often create much press comment.

Valuation objectives (market capitalisation)

Professional investors whose objective was to value the company assessed the traditional financial accounting information to be more relevant. However, regardless of their objective, professional investors assess information in the income statement to be significantly more useful than information in the balance sheet. They also use external information and a restricted set of KPIs (such as the number of subscribers, devices [e.g. iPhone] sales etc.).

Performance of management (growth and long-term profitability)

Financial accounting information is less relevant. However, individual items on the profit-and-loss or income statement were viewed as more important, but the investors still want the overall financial reports.

To assess managerial performance, these investors, interested in the performances of management, rely on KPIs and alternative performance measures. The report found that such alternative information sources are sometimes obtained directly from the firm and from third-party sources. Such sources include qualitative and quantitative non-financial information about the firm and its management, information about the industry and competitors, information about product markets, and, to a lesser degree, information about corporate governance and the general macro-economic environment.

So these investors want to focus on information that reflects managerial effort and tend to discard information that is relevant for the value of a firm but is beyond the control of management, such as macro-induced valuation gains and losses of financial instruments or in pension liabilities.

Investors who are more interested in this objective view the corporate governance of a firm as highly influential and more important than the representational faithfulness of financial reporting. This group also attached significantly more weight to accounting information for stewardship purposes compared with company valuation. So the balance sheet becomes more important – that and the ability to pay consistent dividends.

The three objectives (market capitalisation, performance of management and stewardship) are spread along a spectrum. There are an infinite number of possibilities between these three and other objectives.

Where are we now?

There are two takeaways from this chapter. Firstly, there is no longer a single objective for a company. Instead, multiple and sometimes conflicting objectives are the new normal for companies. Different valuation methods suit differing objectives. The second takeaway is that no single valuation method or set of standards can cover all the possible conflicting objectives. Differing objectives might dictate differing valuation methods and standards. 'One size fits all' is no longer appropriate. Even the FRC[27] accepts that the composition of the reports in future reporting networks might look very different. That said different valuation methods require properly justification and explanation. It would be too easy to choose the valuation meeting just management's objective. So there must a level of independent assurance for the justification and explanations of any valuation method used.

Notes

1 J. Flower, *Accounting and Distributive Justice*, Routledge 2010, page 182.
2 See for example Berle-Means thesis, available at: www.businessdiction-ary.com/definition/Berle-Means-thesis.html, accessed July 2020. Or https://en.wikipedia.org/wiki/The_Modern_Corporation_and_Private_Property.
3 D. Cumming, Investors must hold bad bosses to account, *The Sunday Times*, 25 August 2019, available at: www.thetimes.co.uk/article/investors-must-hold-bad-bosses-to-account-qlh92qpgg, accessed August 2019.
4 B. Martin, Is private equity good for British business? *The Times*, 21 September 2020, available at: www.thetimes.co.uk/article/is-private-equity-good-for-british-business-0wbwhsl3q, accessed September 2020.
5 A. Edgecliffe-Johnson, Companies under pressure to declare 'social purpose', *Financial Times*, 22 August 2019, available at: www.ft.com/content/7ba44ea8-c4f7-11e9-a8e9-296ca66511c9, accessed August 2019.
6 R. Henderson and P. Temple-West, Group of US corporate leaders ditches shareholder-first mantra, *Financial Times*, 19 August 2019, available at: www.ft.com/content/e21a9fac-c1f5-11e9-a8e9-296ca66511c9, accessed August 2019.
7 Manufactured by Foxconn and others.
8 *Financial Times*, 2019, available at: https://aboutus.ft.com/en-gb/new-agenda/, accessed June 2020.
9 L. Barber, Capitalism. Times for a resent. This is the new agenda, *Financial Times*, 19 September 2019, available at: https://aboutus.ft.com/en-gb/new-agenda/, accessed September 2019.
10 Editorial Board, Business must act on a new corporate purpose. Companies must realign incentives and define targets beyond profits, *Financial Times*, 19 September 2019, available at: www.ft.com/content/3732eb04-c28a-11e9-a8e9-296ca66511c9?segmentId=839af127-9a56-c30f-330c-43e43f9e73eb, accessed September 2019.

11 R. Foroohar, The age of wealth accumulation is over. Voters and politicians agree
    it is time to slice the economic pie more evenly, *Financial Times*, 4 August 2019,
    available at: www.ft.com/content/fd13020e-b502-11e9-bec9-fdcab53d6959?
    segmentId=56a414e9-1544-b801-9546-2d038c8b8694, accessed September 2019.
12 Op. Cit. Financial Times, 2019.
13 Op. Cit. Barber, 2019.
14 Op. Cit. Editorial Board, 2019.
15 Op. Cit. Foroohar, 2019.
16 G. Tett, Does capitalism need saving from itself? *Financial Times*, 6 Sep-
    tember 2019, available at: www.ft.com/content/b35342fe-cda4-11e9-99a4-
    b5ded7a7fe3f?segmentId=9d8c66e5-f845-1254-610a-f597ecc6b8b8, accessed
    September 2019.
17 Wikipedia, EU illegal state aid case against Apple in Ireland, available at: https://
    en.wikipedia.org/wiki/EU_illegal_state_aid_case_against_Apple_in_Ireland,
    accessed December 2020.
18 Federation of European Accountants (FEE) Cogito Paper, the future of cor-
    porate reporting, 2015, available at: www.accountancyeurope.eu/wp-content/
    uploads/12_ACCA_Future_of_Corporate_Reporting_draft_response.pdf,
    accessed June 2020.
19 In fact, Rolls-Royce Holdings reported comprehensive losses of more than
    £2 billion in both 2018 and 2019, and then the company experienced a drastic fall
    in revenues due to the airline industry being badly affected by the coronavirus.
20 Accounting for new business models, *Economica*, April 2018, available at:
    https://economia.icaew.com/en/features/april-2018/accounting-for-new-
    business-models, accessed April 2018.
21 Sliced and Diced, Upstart meal-kit companies may need a new recipe for
    growth, *The Economist*, 14 April 2018, available at: www.economist.com/
    news/business/21740450-competition-supermarket-chains-eating-their-profits-
    upstart-meal-kit-companies-may, accessed May 2018.
22 FRC, The future of corporate reporting: A matter of principle, FRC Discus-
    sion paper, *FRC News*, 8 October 2020, available at: https://www.frc.org.uk/
    getattachment/cf85af97-4bd2-4780-a1ec-dc03b6b91fbf/Future-of-Corporate-
    Reporting-FINAL.pdf, accessed October 2020.
23 FRC, The results of the FRC's initial survey from the online survey of FRC
    Stakeholders on the future of Corporate Reporting, *FRC News*, 8 October 2020,
    p. 21, available at: https://www.frc.org.uk/getattachment/97c4336c-3cf2-4884-
    8bcf-1f9542572669/Survey-report-final.pdf, accessed October 2020.
24 ICAS & EFRAG, Multiple authors, professional investors and the deci-
    sion usefulness of financial, reporting, 2016, available at: www.researchgate.
    net/profile/Stefano_Cascino/publication/301637375_Professional_Investors_
    and_the_Decision_Usefulness_of_Financial_Reporting/links/571f507108
    aed056fa23308f/Professional-Investors-and-the-Decision-Usefulness-of-
    Financial-Reporting.pdf?origin=publication_detail, accessed June 2020.
25 https://hbr.org/2017/04/good-management-predicts-a-firms-success-better-
    than-it-rd-or-even-employee-skills.
26 The Economist, DeFANGed? Big tech is growing, but so is investors' caution,
    26 April 2018, available at: www.economist.com/news/business/21741189-
    years-american-tech-giants-were-treated-single-asset-class-no-more-big-tech,
    accessed June 2020.
27 Op. Cit FRC 2020, The future of corporate reporting.

9 Reporting for the post-pandemic future

How to cope with the differing objectives in the longer run

The impact of the COVID-19 pandemic on reporting will be significant: the larger-than-expected downturn of economic activity, 'the uncertainty about the further development of the pandemic and the widespread effect on sales, supply chain and financial markets and other areas add significant uncertainties to the financial results and outlooks which need careful consideration in investor communication'.[1] That rather understates the case with debt by UK companies heading towards £100+ billion and similar amounts of new equity. It could even be much higher. (UK government net borrowing is heading towards £250 billion [£215 billion by the end of November 2020]). One might even venture to say that nothing will be the same again – a new normalcy with a focus on risk and uncertainty is likely to become the norm.

Risk versus uncertainty

Risk assessment has been with us for some time. Risk can be said to be an uncertain event with chances of occurrence that can be predicted and measured. Uncertainty is an uncertain event whereby the chances of occurrence cannot be predicted and measured. COVID-19 is an example of an uncertain event when examining the future in 2020. The possible outcomes were not predictable or quantifiable before the coronavirus hit globally. Even post-pandemic they are not. So 'uncertainty' assessment takes us into a new reporting development. We think it important to separate risk and uncertainty in separate reports.

Assumptions

Let us assume that there exists advanced IT systems and specialised reporting AI systems familiar with the underlying raw or semi-structured data and imbued with multiple valuation rules and multiple accounting rules. Such assisted AI systems will aid anyone with suitable permissions to extract data. Add to these assumptions is the important issue the aftermath post-pandemic of 2020 – especially stretching into 2021 and beyond. Even if the vaccines work efficiently, the post-pandemic economy will suffer markedly and cause as yet unknown economic damage. The issue of 'going concern' and (the longer-run) viability will be treated more seriously: the aftermath of job reductions, collapsing retail high streets, knock-on effects on manufacturing, and rising unemployment in the pandemic's wake. In addition, the public perceptions will change – what is regarded as private will change. Generations Y, Z, and beyond will have a different view compared with Baby Boomers and Generation X persons. This is discussed in Appendix 3.09.1.

Possible framework for professional and institutional investors

We believe that one set of financial statements cannot meet the objectives of all the groups of professional or institutional investors. This is our working assumption and also lately the FRC's.[2] And we have found that one uniform valuation method is not necessarily appropriate. For comparative purposes, we agree that there should be at least one universal standard for the CORE report; but others may form part of the CORE report with subtable justification (and that justification being confirmed by the auditors as valid). However, it is clear that fair value/mark-to-market, historical cost, and current value all have their place.

As with Rolls-Royce, a financial case might be made to have more than one set of accounts based on different valuation criteria – subject to an external check from the auditors. It may be appropriate to have the IFRS valuation in the CORE report with three sets of summary accounts for each group of reporting objectives, with detailed financial statements, reconciliation, and explanations in three separate MORE reports. That is probably going too far, as we may be able to segment reports to their primary investor focus.

Remember, too, that we have to be aware that a wider set of stakeholders will use these reports. So we need some balance. A market capitalisation growth company might have to produce something more mundane for its wider set of stakeholders.

Revenue recognition under multiple reporting objectives

As we saw earlier, the recognition of revenue under IFRS 15 companies only allows the recognition of revenues when they are actually received. This is not necessarily appropriate for all business models. See Box 9.1.

Box 9.1   Revenue recognition under multiple reporting objectives

Early revenues and later expenditure

(To illustrate this forcefully we have moved back in time. So please assume/pretend this scenario takes us back to early 2018.) Software companies and companies selling intellectual property generally have early revenues and later expenditure. Tesla has probably received more than 500,000 deposits of $1,000 for their lower-priced Model 3 but production is pitifully slow (only 16,000 for 2017 and up to March 2018). In these cases, revenue recognition should be spread over several years.

Later revenue and early expenditure

For example, subscription companies, Rolls-Royce, construction companies, and indeed Carillion. In these cases, a proportion of revenue not yet paid might be brought forward.

In theory, we like the concept of being able to have a set of accounts produced under different valuation models. For the report users, this could be with the consent of the external auditors, as we commented earlier. In practice, we think we probably have to restrict the number of choices.

The financial statements and other information in the CORE report might include:

1   A central IFRS – based set of financial statements obeying all current accounting standards, regulations, guidelines, and laws

2   A set of standard reports using one or two (preferably) of the bases of the three objectives already stated (if different from item 1):

   a   Performance of management as epitomised by growth (revenue and profit)

   b   Stewardship equating to maintenance of assets and perhaps modest but steady dividends. Emphasis on assets and liquidity

   c   Share valuation where market capitalisation and its growth are all that matters and, as a secondary consideration, the value of net assets.

Any one of these or all three sets would be subject to some external assurance but maybe not comprise a full audit.

3   A set of measures that identifies the most important conventional financial figures and KPIs and APMs relevant to each class of objectives and externally audited to the secondary (as defined

in item c above) external audit standard, also encompassing any industry or sector KPIs in common use or offered by third parties. Appendix 3.09.2 discusses KPI and other measures in hotels and coffee shops.

4   The availability of raw or semi-structured data that can be used by professional investors to undertake self-service the type of reports based on whatever valuation method they choose. This would be deduced with the aid of an AI assistant (provided by the firm in question with knowledge of the firm's underlying data and conversant with a variety of different valuation and accounting rules). Such reports tailored and pulled from granular data would not be audited and would be used at the investors' risk. But the AI would be able to testify to the level of accuracy.

Possible framework for preparers in the long term

We propose that preparers can produce in the CORE financial reporting system as follows, but some of this, such as the forecasting model and data and assumptions, will be kept on the website (but subject to audit or a level of reassurance). The full set of components of the financial statement section is shown in Appendix 3.09.3.

In this appendix we also map the proposed FRC structure in their future of corporate reporting[3] with our framework below. Essentially our CORE report could include the three main FRC network of reports: Financial Statements, Business Report and Public Interest Report. Our scheme equates our CORE report with a subset of the FRC's three reports.

So the structure could become:

CORE report

• Financial statements as per Box 9.2 with the model and assumptions on the website and downloadable in Excel
• Narrative sections (summarised): see next section

MORE financial statements reports

• Alternative valuations and accounting rules producing different sets of accounts in full with reconciliations and explanations in full
• Additional explanations, information, and details of the financial model to produce forecasts. With the model in Excel and all data and assumptions
• Other financial and important non-financial information

MORE reports extensions of the CORE reports

- All the narrative reports – only a summary in the CORE report
- All the committee reports – only a summary in the CORE report
- Other material
- Simulacra and marketing material
- PR material

MORE reports for each class or group of stakeholders including:

- Employees
- Customers
- Suppliers
- Human rights advocates
- Investors
- Lenders and banks
- Environment, sustainability analysts
- Government
- Local and national society and externalities
- Analysts
- Potential investors
- Hedge funds
- Others . . .

Box 9.2 Suggested proposed CORE report for the financial statements

1 UK GAAP/IFRS as modified by our quick fixes with a primary external audit (that is a full and complete audit of all information). Optional: the same set of financial statements produced according to US GAAP (whatever that will become if significantly different from the UK/EU [and we assume it will be]). All to be externally assured in some way.

  a Consolidated income statement
  b Consolidated statement of comprehensive income
  c Consolidated balance sheet (opening, closing, and average)

  Opening, closing, and preferably two other time periods (but at least one) to provide an average balance sheet. We still advocate the opening, closing, and average balance sheets. For the CORE annual report:

d   Consolidated cash flow statement
e   Consolidated statement of changes in equity
f   Notes to the consolidated financial statements
g   And other information as per current and future regulations.

2   A set of financial statements but using a preferred valuation method and accounting rules, to better show the true underlying nature of the business – if permitted by the external auditors. For example, they could adopt different revenue recognition schemes. The differences could be explained and a resolution between IFRS and their favoured revenue recognition shown. Both sets would be externally audited to the most complete auditing standard whatever that becomes.

3   To be agreed with the external auditors, a minimum set of KPIs and APMs relevant to the company or group and the industries in which it operates. These to be assured.

4   A 10-year history as per quick fix. Tertiary standard of external reassurance

5   A 7-year forecast (current year plus 6 forecast years) plus a 5-year history with actuals against forecasts shown. These annual forecasts should include:

a   Cash flows
b   Simplified income statement
c   Simplified balance sheet
d   Principle assumptions about exogenous[4] variables and macroeconomic indicators
e   Principle assumptions about endogenous[5] variables (to be explained)
f   Publication of a simplified financial model in an Excel spreadsheet (or equivalent) incorporating a simplified financial model that produces an equivalent forecast to the described data. Together with any assumptions as to exogenous and endogenous variables. All physical variable assumptions to be stated. These data sets would be included with the published model. If the model changes, a set of reconciliations to previous history should be provided.

6   A set of physical variables that align to the underlying physical variables in the published financial model

7   Notes and reconciliations
8   Shareholder information
9   Subsidiaries and joint ventures
10 Advisers
11 More narrative in non-technical terms about the data
12 Technical notes and glossary of terms used in report

This is not pie-in-the-sky or blue-cloud thinking. Neither are these fixed or inflexible – these are suggestions which can be modified and/or trimmed or expanded upon. We think and believe this is realistic given the progress in technology. We defend our assertions being entirely attainable, reasonable, and feasible as a suggested guide for the way forward. In Appendix 3.09.3 (Possible framework for preparers in the long term), we provide a proposed set of elements for the CORE report.

CORE narrative and other reports

With possible expansions by the FRC/ARGA new governance code and other additions and extensions – especially risk and uncertainty statements/ assessments – the approach perhaps should be one page per committee and extend this to the remuneration report and independent auditor's report. A one page summary should suffice. Further and full details for each sub-report and committee can occupy a MORE report.

Only the CORE narrative (equivalent to the FRC's Business Report and Public Interest Report – but may be more concise with the greater amount of data in separate sub-reports) and financial statements as described are to be included in the CORE report as a single entity on a website and also downloadable as a single PDF file and Excel file or equivalent. Wherever possible, Excel files or equivalent should be available on the site and for download. Also when downloading a set, the default naming convention should include the name of the company, the type of report, and the year. So many companies still do not do this.

All other MORE reports can be shown on the website with a possible PDF download facility. A level of assurance should be attached to each.

Separate out the sustainability and environment report into a MORE report. For the CORE report, produce one-page summaries if possible (order not important) and then the detail in further MORE. Not every firm will want to populate all the headings that follow; however, these are a suggested possible list:

Strategy
Vision and business model (more detailed optional)
Objectives and constraints (as defined earlier and more detailed optional).
Markets and products/services
Our principle competitors
Our resources
Sustainability and environment (enhanced over current in a MORE report)
Business overview

> Overall performance review including such issues as market share, sales volumes, pricing mix, expansion, or contraction

What diverged from the plans during the year (new)

> We would like to see a statement forcing management to identify events and performance that did not go to plan or was below budget or standard.

What went right during the year; better than planned? (new)

> We would like to see a statement forcing management to identify events and performance that went better than planned or budgeted.

Unexpected events or issues (new)

> We think it would be useful to identify any factors or circumstances which affected the performance or otherwise of the company during the year being reported on.

Financial highlights/overview and APMs
Chairman's statement
Chief executive's statement/review
Divisional performance (if necessary); several pages
KPIs and non-financial information (as relevant)
New investment, acquisitions, mergers, and takeovers
Human resources
Employees
Subcontractors and/or contractors
Suppliers
Supply chain
Human rights, slavery, and child labour
Customers
Marketing and PR – several pages
Financial review – possibly two pages
Principle risk and uncertainties
Risk assessment (briefly with a fuller report in MORE)

Uncertainty assessment and stress testing (briefly with a fuller report in
  MORE)
Going-concern report over the next 12 months
Viability and survivability longer-term report
Financial model details and explanations
Profit and cash-flow forecasts

  Summary of cash-flow forecast and explanation

Viability report covering the next 7 years or possibly 7 years
Corporate citizenship and public interest
Externalities report (possibly)
Governance
Board of directors
Audit committee report
Summary of communications between external auditors and the audit
  committee
Shareholder complaints as per the new governance code (forthcoming)
Nomination committee and remuneration policy report
Remuneration report (possibly combined with above)
Independent/external auditor's report
Financial statements (several pages)

  using CORE assumptions, accounting rules, and valuation methods
  guide and summary to alternative financial statements

Summary of guide to notes
Shareholder information
List of subsidiaries and ownership levels
History (10-year record)
Glossary

A CORE report for the non-institutional investors, shareholders, and stakeholders needs to be simplified and geared towards the non-expert, using where
possible a set of common terms and layouts – as shown in Appendix 3.09.3.

Narrative reports

Solutions to neutralise and give a really balanced appraisal of the business
in the narrative section of reports, we believe, require some sort of independent assessment. These are explored in Appendix 3.09.4. In this appendix, we deal with a variety of possible ways of coping with problems of
biased narrative reports or those written in a way to influence in a more
positive way than could be justified neutrally.

About the financial and cash-flow models

The coronavirus and the latest financial failures have given rise to more importance for the going-concern and viability statements – not only those provided by management but also those given the seal of approval by the auditors. So we postulate that there should be several sets of forecasting models.

1   One that the firm uses and might be made available to professional investors with or without management's assumptions and forecast exogenous variables.
2   The second would be a simplified one made available to all and published in the CORE report and on the website with all the simplified assumptions and exogenous variables and data. This would allow any stakeholder to run the model with their own assumptions and perform their own sensitivity analysis and stress tests.

> We think that we should probably enforce no questioning of the model, the assumptions, any exogenous data, or the results except by the auditors (obviously) and at the AGM. Otherwise we could imagine management time taken up with many questions on the model, the modelling process, and the assumptions.

So the actual forecasting model used by the company in its published forecast may be based on a more complicated model. The one that is published for users to run can be much simplified. However, it should be capable of producing a similar forecast (say a profit or turnover figure within 10% or so for at least 3 years out). If the model cannot, then there should be an adjustment factor and some explanations of why the two models could not produce results within the 10% margin.

Of the elements in a forecast, the most important element is the cash-flow forecast. We have used the term 'physical variables'. By that we mean items such as units of production, units of sales; these might be by type or line, sector/segment, operating units, or broken down into something that makes sense for that particular company. It also would encompass raw material costs of the same items, headcount by classes of wage range, and the price cost data on a unit basis. Of course, some companies, services, would need to fashion a typical project (e.g. a building project) and then gross up from that typical project. Cost would be subject to a mix variation. Prices too – if there is a more expensive set of products or services being sold, then that would be a higher unit price and perhaps margins.

This is not a book about financial modelling, so we are not going to dwell on the mechanics. However, we believe that every director on a board should be capable of building and running a financial model – however simple.

In addition, understanding the financial consequences when the financial model is stress tested and systematic sensitivity analysis is undertaken.

What we have done is to provide more information about financial models for forecasts in Appendix 3.09.5. We explore the fundamentals of the basic set of variables, and financial parameters are specified. These are presented in this appendix (Whitbread revenue buildup for financial modelling and forecasting purposes) with links to other sites. This uses Whitbread as an example when it owned both Costa Coffee and the Premier Inn hotel chain. In this appendix, we focus on the build-up of the revenue figures of Whitbread's Premier Inn hotel division, and the Costa Coffee division provides some flesh from which a financial model could be derived. The accuracy of forecasts is considered in Appendix 9.03.6.

NEDs to develop their own spreadsheet models

We also suggest that each NED (non-executive director) run and document their own version of the simplified model with their assumptions and stress tests. These should be documented in board meetings and available for the external auditors to examine. If these are not run properly with differing assumptions, then this should be stated in the annual report under the name of each non-executive director via a statement such as, 'We certify that XX non-executive director has undertaken a range of forecasts under different assumptions from that of management and have performed some stress tests'.

The auditors should check that these assumptions are sensible and ensure they show a range of forecasts which are different from those of management. They might also say something like 'When interviewing the non-executive director on these forecasts, XX has shown an understanding of the relationship between the variables and the possible impact of profits, assets, cash inflows, cash outflows, and net borrowing and finance requirements. They are aware of any funding problems discovered in the process of understanding their forecasts and sensitivity analysis, including their own personal stress test'.

Other communications

Distress messaging signalling a change in strategy

Companies may have to make distress messages to fend off the effect of activist shareholders on company decisions and reports. The recent (2018/9) case of Whitbread and shareholder pressure to hive off a major subsidiary (Costa Coffee) meant the Whitbread board felt the need to bring forward the divestment decision and make a public statement, which is certainly, a 'disruption' to the normal internal decision making process.

Whitbread as an example

The reason we used Whitbread as an example earlier is that we feel strongly that there are certain negative features to current capital markets. We liked the original company's strategy. We liked their report. We think they were doing well, although the margins on the hotel business were much higher than the coffee business. Then along came two US-based hedge funds – Sachem Head and Elliot Advisers (the latter mentioned by Wikipedia as a vulture fund[6]). The latter also built up a shareholding of 6% prior to a possible takeover bid. To us, Whitbread was a healthy and growing company with an impressive long-term strategy.

Alison Brittain, Whitbread's chief executive, had to give way in the face of a possible takeover bid. So she announced the sale of the Costa Coffee division to head off such a bid. However, the two hedge funds wanted a sale within six months; Allison Brittan wanted to finish development and sell Costa within 2 years. In the end, Whitbread sold Costa Coffee to Coca-Cola for a good price (£3.9 billion) ahead of their CEO's desired timetable.

Alison Brittain had previously declared herself open to the idea of a sale but maintained that both businesses needed more investment first. After announcing the demerger, she said, 'We have always said you wouldn't sell your house at a time when you've got the roof off and you're doing all the rewiring – and that is what we are doing at the moment'.

The reasons for the pressure for splitting the assets and then selling the Costa Coffee division, retaining the Premier Inns, are:

1   Elliott's position is understood to be that Costa should be a separate entity from the Whitbread group, as Costa and Premier Inn are largely run as separate businesses with minimal overlap in the management teams – something that need not be the case. They argue that Whitbread is trading at a discount as one corporate entity, and creating a standalone Costa would boost the value of both relatively painlessly by up to 40%, or £3 billion – in the end, Whitbread got £3.9 billion, which, in our view, is an exceptionally good price.

2   Scott Ferguson, managing partner at Sachem Head, told a hedge fund conference in New York why he thought Costa would be better off as an independent business: 'When management no longer has a big brother to lean on, problems tend to be solved'. The authors disagree; there is no evidence that this is so, especially if the spin-off is saddled with debt.

3   Laith Khalaf, a senior analyst at the investment company Hargreaves Lansdown, said, 'Coffee shops and hotel rooms don't make natural bedfellows, so splitting off Costa Coffee from Premier Inn makes sense for Whitbread'. We disagree. Both serve drinks and food snacks as well as some commonality with meals. There is enormous scope for economies of scale in supply and also in distribution logistics. Cross-brand loyalty schemes are also possibilities as well as cross-pollination of online sites. Provisional analysis by the authors put this advantage to be as much as 23p per cup of coffee. In terms of savings in hotel rooms, this comes to significantly more. We believe that our numerical estimates show that hotels and coffee bars do make good bedfellows.

See Appendix 3.09.7 (Distress messaging signalling a change in strategy) for a full list of references and any further comments and analysis we may have on this issue. What the Whitbread management may have done in staving off a takeover bid is to redistribute overhead allocation to balance the returns (if warranted) rather than have the hotel group very much more profitable than Costa. That said, we do not know the underlying details.

Entropy and messaging

The value of a message or the informational content can be varied depending on circumstances. Often it is the unexpected message or information that has most value terms for decision making (i.e. buy or sell shares). The message 'it is going to rain today' means vastly more, if accurate, in the Sahara desert than in the UK. Entropy and the informational content of messaging is further discussed in Appendix 3.09.8. We postulate an entropy measure for forecasts, with illustrative examples in Appendix 3.09.8a.

The issue of how to obtain consistency in the longer term in reporting is discussed in Appendix 3.09.9.

Delivery systems

At the moment, the annual report is either on paper or downloadable as a PDF file on the web. Those are the two audited documents. Other pieces of information on the web or interim reports, messages, or announcements are not audited. However, this may change. Increasingly we believe that the delivery system, of the MORE reports and other isolated but important pieces of data (e.g. number of users) might be reported on the company's website alone. The main CORE report can always be a PDF file. There needs to be a hierarchy of level of assurance for the increased information in the numerous MORE reports. External audit will, we advocate, have to cover some of the MORE reports on the website.

Within our time frame, we envisage:

- AI assistants and systems will be providing and interpreting the complete reporting environments. So extracting anything may involve interactions with the AI assistant and helper. Even to obtain the main CORE report and any standard MORE report will require interaction with the AI to understand the structure of the reports and to extract the most relevant one for the user and then to present it in a form that the 'user' likes together with any newly created graphs or tables – sometimes drawing upon additional data.
- Depending on permissions and privileges, some users may extract their information requirements from the raw or semi-structured data via a self-service application or AI system.
- Reporting of relevant information will be tailored to each class of user or stakeholder and possibly to each person who takes the time to define certain parameters – given sufficient permissions and privileges.
- The information will be received by your computer, smart watch/pen, your glasses, your wearable, or, just possibly, that 'old-fashioned' but much-enhanced smartphone.
- Those devices might then pass this information to the user directly to one's ears, eyes, and even possibly directly to one's mind (discussed below). We know that it is probable that this will move from paper to electronic and web based. It is even possible, in the long term, for there to be direct input to the brain; Elon Musk's company Neuralink is developing such a technique, for example,[7] but that is in the very long term.

The intangibles issue

The period 2018 to 2021 has been a record one for mergers and takeovers. The FTSE 100, discussed earlier in Chapter 3 (and Appendix 3.03.1/2) will be very different by 2021 and then again in 2022. Many of the famous names of the FTSE 100 (such as GKN, Shire, EasyJet, British Gas, and even ITV) will have been taken over (possibly broken up) or suffered a reduction in their share price.[8] In Chapter 4, we highlighted the problem of intangible assets (also discussed in Appendix 3.04.13).

Differentiation intangible types

Type 1 'value' less than their balance sheet numbers

As we saw in Carillion, intangibles formed a major part of the balance sheet. That is not unusual. Our research indicates that about 80% of the assets of leading non-tech businesses are intangible in nature and that many are nowhere near their balance sheet value. Every time a takeover happens, there will normally be an additional entry in intangible assets (normally under acquisition Goodwill). Though in theory the current safety valve is that an impairment review should be included routinely on acquisition goodwill. So the hectic takeover activity in the last few years and currently (new records being set) will lead to a larger set of intangible assets – many of which, as in Carillion, are not worth their book value in the balance sheet. Not every merger or takeover brings the wished-for synergies or benefits.

Type 2 market capitalisation greater than the total balance sheet asset value

However, there is the parallel and reverse phenomenon – the tech giants and start-ups, the unicorns, and successful disruptive companies (such as Tesla, Uber, Airbnb, Deliveroo, Snowflake, Doordash, etc.) are worth far more in market capitalisation than their balance sheet values. So there is a serious mismatch and possible reporting black hole. This type of intangible issue is characterised by high market capitalisation or P/E ratios that are massive. Such values are basically concerned with expectations or potential futures, or even forecasts of what might happen. Such characteristics might also determine how we might treat this phenomenon.

Increasing divergence between book and market values

For both types, one can observe the increasing divergence between book and market values and partially attribute that to information that is outside of the financial report. For Type 2, this can also attribute some of the gap to non-financial information either within the report itself or released to the market in other ways (press statements, on the website, and by third-party industry watchers or analysts).

The stock market value of the firm and its actual performance bear little resemblance to any conventional valuation formula. Multiples of profits or potential profits are sky high. Companies which make a loss can still be valued in billions. Often, as we said earlier, non-financial information (the product, subscribers, users, visitors, services delivered) are much more important than the pure financial statements. This type of non-financial information is important in the forecasting and modelling process, just as volume or changes in the shopping basket are for manufacturers/retailers.

For the social media companies and chat apps, what is important is the number and growth in those subscribers (with a view to selling advertising fees for access to those subscribers). As of 2020, Twitter fails with only 330 million., whilst WhatsApp (1.5 billion), Messenger (1.3 billion) and Instagram (1 billion) were bought by Facebook for enormous sums.[9] They all had rapidly growing subscribers, whereas Twitter had little growth. Tencent owns the fast growing, QQ, WeChat, and Qzone (mainly Chinese). ByteDance owns TikTok, which has a rapidly growing number of subscribers (around 1 billion) but has been the source of political intrigue with former President Trump.

Resolution

We believe that it should be accepted that the intangibles question will not be resolved through strict conventional financial reporting. Instead, it is part of the broader approach to reporting that looks beyond historical financial performance and deals with forward-looking statements and forecasts. One possibility is if companies can report authenticated (via blockchains or some other similar secure filing/ledger system) historical cash flow information on a disaggregated basis, does this permit valuations based on a more granular (albeit historical) set of data? And will this work to narrow the intangibles gap? Perhaps for Type 1 but not for Type 2 – the latter relies more on non-financial information and forecasts.

However, there is no clarity as to what external information is a driver of value, and there may be considerable differences between industry sectors. They rightly say that there is also a lot of noise, which may result in the information being visible only to those with the tools and skills to cut through the fog.

Type 1 scenarios

For Type 1, where the real value (sales value, discounted cash-flow net present value, breakup value, asset value in a forced sale, etc.) is less than the balance sheet, more light could be shed if there was some attempt to evaluate the real (and lower) worth of these divisions in a separate report – possibly audited. For those companies which have goodwill but have been completely integrated into the company doing the taking over, it may be more difficult to provide any basis for separate valuation. However, there should be a note on the contribution to current profitability in both non-financial and financial terms.

Type 2 scenarios

For Type 2, where the market capitalisation exceeds the balance sheet value, we propose that this should have a reconciliation-to-market value report. This should contain:

a   The critical non-financial information should be published and a justi-
    fication why these variables(s) are important.
b   A valuation model that links market capitalisation or share price to the
    non-financial information in item a. This could be statistically by some
    simple formula such as least squares, a more complex econometric
    model, or other statistical or logical processes. It might be formed from
    a simple deterministic model.[10]
c   A reconciliation between a and b back 2 or 3 years.

Where are we now?

Our central thesis is not to have one integrated report but a hybrid system in which there is a single CORE report (which could contain the FRC's main network of reports – though perhaps shortened) and a number of MORE reports. We draw attention to the fact that the FRC is suggesting major change to reporting – with flexibility and adaptation to changing needs and events. Much of what the FRC suggest we would agree with. The one area of divergence is that one set of reports meets all the needs of stakeholders and users. We feel different classes of stakeholders will be interested in different information. We also go further in the use of multiple valuation methods and an emphasis on forward looking statements, forecast and predictions. We also add financial models and forecasts in a more major way.

Risks about known events and uncertainty (of the unknown, i.e. the pandemic) are contrasted. The conclusion is that there should be a set of financial models (published) with assumptions. Sensitivity and stress testing with a range of outcomes should be published, with any changes and discrepancies over time explained. We are also advocating that the independent NEDs run their own simplified models to assure themselves of the survivability of the company. Messaging between the company and anyone should be better documented and subject to tests including a content and entropy measure. Lastly, the divergence between the balance sheet and market capitalisation needs to be documented, and an attempt to explain any differences. This is the case in which intangibles have to be written down – but by which valuation method? Probably more than one with alternative assumptions. The more significant case is where market capitalisation far exceeds the balance sheet value. This needs ratifying and documenting – not something to be swept under the carpet from a reporting system designed in an age gone by. The situation over the next 50 years is going to provide many challenges, opportunities, and, above all, changes. The events of the last few years show that change is inevitable.

Notes

1 How COVID-19 infects financial reporting and results presentations, *Deloitte Website*, 2020, available at: https://www2.deloitte.com/ch/en/pages/audit/articles/financial-reporting-survey-q1-2020.html, accessed September 2020.

2 FRC, The results of the FRC's initial survey from the online survey of FRC Stakeholders on the future of Corporate Reporting, *FRC News*, 8 October 2020, available at: https://www.frc.org.uk/getattachment/97c4336c-3cf2-4884-8bcf-1f9542572669/Survey-report-final.pdf, accessed October 2020.

3 FRC, The future of corporate reporting discussion paper, *FRC News*, 8 October 2020, available at: https://www.frc.org.uk/news/october-2020/frc-publishes-future-of-corporate-reporting-discus, accessed October 2020; and FRC, The future of corporate reporting discussion paper, *FRC News*, 8 October 2020, available at: https://www.frc.org.uk/news/october-2020/frc-publishes-future-of-corporate-reporting-discus, accessed October 2020.

4 Having an external cause or origin – not something which can be controlled by management.

5 Something that can be controlled or influenced by management.

6 Available at: https://en.wikipedia.org/wiki/Elliott_Management_Corporation, accessed September 2020.

7 See their website www.neuralink.com/.

8 Similarly, GE, Exxon-Mobil, Pfizer, and Raytheon were dropped from the Dow Jones Industrial Average.

9 Currently the subject of US anti-trust actions which may force the breakup of these constituent parts of Facebook.

10 Uber provided a cogent argument in its IPO, citing 14 million trips a day and $78 billion paid to drivers with the possibility of 10+ billion trips.